Remember Me
As You Pass By

Remember Me As You Pass By

Stories from Prairie Graveyards

Nancy Millar

GLENBOW
MUSEUM • ART GALLERY • LIBRARY • ARCHIVES

Alberta Treasury Branches
Guaranteed Financial Services

Glenbow is grateful to Alberta Treasury Branches
for its generous sponsorship and enthusiastic support
of this publication.

Canadian Cataloguing in Publication Data

Millar, Nancy

Remember me as you pass by: stories from prairie graveyards

ISBN 1-895379-26-1

1. Cemeteries - Alberta - History. 2. Funeral rites and ceremonies -
Alberta. 3. Burial - Alberta. I. Glenbow Museum II. Title

GT3213.M45 1994 393'.1'097123 C94-900574-6

Acknowledgements

Special thanks to all the people who gave me directions, answered my questions, looked up historical information, wandered through graveyards on my behalf, did whatever they could to help me write this book. I appreciated the assistance and the friendliness over and over again.

Special thanks to Beth Duthie who applied the magic of editing to my script. It made all the difference.

Special thanks to Glenbow and Donna Livingstone for putting the words between covers.

And finally, special thanks to my family who, as ever, supported me in more ways than one!

Contents

An Introduction

"Remember me as you pass by
So as you are, so once was I.
As I am now so soon you'll be,
Prepare for death and eternity."

...on the gravemarker of William Henry Erichson,
1859-1927, in the Gadsby Cemetery

For three summers now, I have tramped through a lot of graveyards — not a particularly normal thing to do, I know. Had I climbed flagpoles and eaten worms while at the top, I would not have been regarded with such suspicion. But to wander through graveyards, that is truly weird in a world that has a lot of ways to be weird, so I'd better explain. I did so because of an old graveyard in Canmore and a pile of rocks in central Alberta. Truly.

Canmore is a pleasant mountain town on the edge of Banff National Park. Part of it wants to be big and rich like Switzerland; part of it wants to be small and modest like Canmore. Its graveyard is tucked away beneath three great big hoodoos — nicer sentinels I can't think of — and is fenced by mountains. No need in this graveyard for tall monuments made of granite. What else are mountains for?

At first sight, the graveyard itself looks pretty standard—rows of markers and trees and a rather dilapidated statue of a soldier in the Field of Honour. It's neat and tidy but not particularly memorable until you spot the old cemetery at the back, and then you know you've found something even better than the hoodoos. Years ago, town officials gave up trying to sort out who was buried where in the original cemetery, so they just fenced it off and started anew. The new part is what you see out front, the part that looks like most other cemeteries, but the old part, hidden away behind trees and a fence, is something else again, an absolutely wonderful tangle of life and death, light and dark, old and new. I was completely charmed when I found it, and although I didn't realize it

1

at the moment, I was hooked on the feelings and stories that can be experienced in such a place.

It's the growth that you see first in the old part—wild roses and saskatoon bushes, grass and poplar trees, old spruce trees with boughs that bend to the ground, new ones whose branches reach to the sky. Then you see the wooden picket fences surrounding many of the original graves. For the children, the fences are small, like little boxes. For the adults, they're bed size. When the fences are made of wrought iron — and a lot are — they even look like old-fashioned beds. The wrought iron ones are holding their shape, but the wooden ones have begun to lean, often as a unit, as if a meeting had been held and the angle of lean agreed upon for the year. Others have fallen over, only to be held up by nearby trees or a neighbouring fence. This is a very cooperative cemetery: fences and markers help one another where they can; where they can't, nature steps in and holds or covers or disguises. No one paints the wooden pickets anymore, so nature has done its best with sun and storm to make them all a sort of pearly grey, the wood worn right down to its bones but strong still and standing.

Inside the fences are the gravemarkers — some marble, a few metal, a few wooden ones that have survived — and because they were placed there at a time when words were expected on a gravemarker, they tell stories. Not very long ones or very complete ones, but stories that make you want to turn the pages back to the beginning of the book. Add the occasional bouquet of plastic roses and you're hooked. At least I was. This is how it happened.

Inside one of the boxlike picket fences was a white marble cross. I could tell by its size that it probably marked a child's grave, and sure enough, when I pushed the rose bush and grass out of the way of the inscription, I found: **"Nelio, son of Serofino and Emma Vola, born Aug. 22, 1910, died Nov. 2, 1910."** There was no more than that, no indication of why this two-month-old child might have died. But as I moved the grass back into place, I noticed a fairly new bouquet of plastic roses at the base of Nelio's grave, right under the words. The bouquet hadn't just blown in from some other grave; it was there by design, the stems of the flowers pushed securely into place. Someone must remember Nelio, I realized, or at least remember the family — his brothers and sisters perhaps? Did he have brothers and sisters, for that matter? And Serofino and Emma — what had become of them? Most of all, who had brought roses to this grave some eighty years later? All that and more I wondered as I stood there on the mountainside looking at the small grave of a small baby. It is such an old-fashioned thing to do, to put flowers on a grave. In this day and age, it's even old-fashioned to have a grave.

I never did find out what happened to Nelio and the Vola family. The local museum has no record of them; old-timers don't recall the name. But after reading the history of Canmore and area, I can guess at his story. Canmore was a mining town in those early days, and a lot of Italian immigrants came as miners. The town grew quickly, sometimes at its peril. For instance, sewage facilities were not always as far removed from water sources as they should have been. Consequently, typhoid fever occurred more often in Canmore than in other towns. That might have accounted for Nelio's death, but it was more likely due to a lack of medical attention at and before birth. Babies died; everyone knew that. When they died in Canmore, more often than not they got a picket fence around their grave, partly to keep the animals off but partly because Canmore had a thriving lumber business. The pickets were available and cheap.

The little marble marker would not have been cheap, however, so Nelio's family must have respected the old world concept of solid and lasting gravemarkers. Not for them a wooden marker that would deteriorate over the years or a metal one that would rust. Instead, they chose the more expensive alternative, which means they either scrimped and saved to mark their young son so well, or else distant members of the family helped with the expense. Burial came with a whole set of religious and societal expectations. It had to be done properly, even if it meant great sacrifices on the part of the living.

The mining operations in Canmore eventually closed, so the Vola family might have moved on to another mining town or another job, who knows? I can't guess at the rest of the story, but I can guess that they visited the little fenced grave before they left. Probably they left flowers, and maybe they said to someone, "Visit our Nelio sometime. Put flowers on his grave for us." And someone did and someone does.

As I researched Nelio and wondered aloud to others around me, I discovered that they, too, were quickly interested in this boy and his short life. There is something compelling about information that comes from a gravemarker, especially when it is accompanied by a mystery like the plastic flowers. "Was there a hospital in Canmore then?" my young niece asked, she who hates anything to do with the formal study of history. "Why did people put fences around graves?" my own grown-up daughter asked, she who thought it was weird of me to be poking about in graveyards. Whether they realized it or not, they were asking historical questions, and it occurred to me that I might be onto something. Maybe I had discovered another way of telling history.

Then I went to a farm in central Alberta to see a pile of rocks.

It was just an ordinary pile of rocks in the middle of a field — rocks and weeds and a little bit of goldenrod beginning to bloom. The field around it was properly summer-fallowed, the lines of the cultivator straight and true until they had to veer around the rocks. "My boys grumble about it," Henry Kemtrup of Dickson admitted to me. "They think it's a nuisance." But they don't know and feel the story like Henry does.

It seems that a young couple moved to this rocky piece of land in the early 1920s. Where they came from, no one knows. They just came. There was a house of some sort on the land but not much else. No roads, no neighbours nearby. Innisfail was about twenty miles east through muskeg and bush. Because the couple arrived in late summer, there was no time to clear land for a crop or garden, so the husband decided to go to Innisfail for a few months to work at the brick plant and make a grubstake for the winter. He would be back before the cold settled in, before the baby was due.

And so it was done. He lived and worked in town; his wife remained behind on the farm. After the first snowfall, he headed home, bringing with him food, supplies, and even some hard cash, and that apparently was his undoing. With incredibly bad luck and timing — for how many strangers would a traveller have met on those nearly invisible trails so many years ago? — he was held up, robbed, and killed. Left in a ditch at the side of the road, a slough still known as Dead Man's Lake.

When the police found him in the spring, after the snow had melted and revealed his body, they rode out to tell his wife. But she had died too, in childbirth. Her twin babies were dead beside her. There was nothing for the police to do but bury the bodies near the farm house and mark the spot with a pile of rocks. And so ended the dream of one young couple who came out west to make a new life for themselves. What a dreadful story of the bad old days.

The rock pile was still there when Henry bought the land in the 1940s, and the story lived on as well. At various times, he and others in the community tried to verify the details, find out the couple's name, learn more about the tragedy, but they had no luck. Police records had been lost, the couple had never formally applied for the land, the brick plant had burned down. Nobody knew, yet everybody knew.

Eventually Henry cleared the land for crops, but he left the rock pile intact. "Every spring when we come to this field, I think of them all alone like that. No family," Henry said. "Must have been terrible."

As we left the field that day, closing the gates behind us, a coyote howled. "He's always there," Henry told me. "It's like he watches over them too." (Incidentally, Henry lost the argument before this book was finished. When last I spoke to him, his sons had moved the rock pile and squared up the field. "They didn't know it like I did," Henry said, "and I couldn't prove anything.")

But it was after my visit with Henry that I knew for sure that I wanted to tell Alberta's past from a different point of view. Instead of starting out with, "So-and-so was born in the year 1883," I wanted to say, "So-and-so is buried under a rock in Henry Kemtrup's back field, and here's the story." Or, "There's a gravemarker in a certain Alberta graveyard that says something unusual, and here's the story." The story, the real person, was the focus of my interest, not the fact of their death and burial. In other words, I wasn't turning into some sort of ghoul; I just wanted to see what I could discover about Alberta's living history from hints gleaned in the graveyard. I wanted to read our history backwards.

It's not as if I was the first person ever to visit a graveyard. People used to do it all the time. It was a Sunday afternoon outing, a way to remember and show respect to those members of the family who had gone before. My husband tells about visiting his Aunt Grace in the grave-yard in Drumheller in the 1940s. His mother would go every Sunday, and he had to come along whether he wanted to or not. It was the right thing to do; he would do it. Also, he would carry the pails of water and the gardening tools that they might need to clean up the grave site.

Once the work was done and he had heard again about Grace and the unfortunate circumstances of her death — antibiotics would have fixed her up in no time — he and his mother headed home. As they walked among the graves on the way to the gate, he would hear about other members of the family who had "passed on" or members of the community who had "gone before." Just because they were in a graveyard didn't mean they were going to use the actual words "death" or "dying."

In contrast, we moderns can say the words without flinching. Certainly we see death every time we turn around — real and fictional in news reports and movies and on television — but just because we hear and see and say the words doesn't mean that death is real for us. The boy who went out to the graveyard on Sundays with his watering can knew more about death than a lot of us who only see it on television or all cleaned up in a funeral home. We have all the words, all the noise and fury signifying death, but we don't visit the graveyard. We don't know our own stories.

Often in a graveyard, with the wind blowing and the ever-present magpies wheeling, I would think about death, not in a morbid way but in a wondering way. It's the last frontier, the one thing we smart human beings know nothing about, and the graveyard is one place where it is right and proper to ponder such imponderables.

That, plus the stories I found, would have been enough to get me started on my journey through prairie graveyards, but then one hot, dry day I was in the Faith Union graveyard south of Etzikom in southeastern Alberta. The prairie grasses were crackling beneath my feet like corn flakes, and the wind — always the wind — sent tumbleweeds spinning across the empty prairie toward the empty sky. How could the first settlers have picked this inhospitable land? How could they have expected crops to grow and flowers to bloom?

It seemed so bleak, this handful of graves with nothing but sky and prairie to keep them company. But just then a meadowlark sang. Its music filled the silence, and it was magic.

That did it. I knew that graveyards would be my project for the next few years: they contain our history and our stories, they make us feel as well as remember, and now and then a meadowlark sings. Who could ask for anything more?

∼

THE LAST WORD: The words on the gravemarker of Eva Leona Hedges Miller, 1885-1970, in the Olds Cemetery offer one possible answer to some of the imponderables:

Ah, that's the reason a bird can sing
On his darkest day, he believes in spring.

~

Community Cemetery in Spedden

Stories of the Babies in Our Graveyards

Sleep on, sweet babe, and take thy rest
God called thee home; He thought it best.

...written on the gravemarker of Vera Elizabeth
Shaw, died Sept. 21, 1906, aged 6 1/2 mos.

The epitaph for Vera Elizabeth is written on the base of her tombstone in the Nanton graveyard. On the top of the stone is a lamb, and as soon as I saw the lamb, I knew that before me was the story of a life that barely got started. I hate finding lambs.

The lamb is both a sacred and a secular symbol. Christians choose it for their children because it symbolizes Jesus Christ, the Lamb of God, who said, "Suffer little children to come unto me." The Bible is full of references to shepherds who watch over their lambs, count them, protect them, so it isn't surprising to find lambs on gravemarkers reminding the Almighty of promises made. Others not so religious select the lamb for their children's gravemarkers because it represents innocence, purity, and youth. One mother that I talked to chose the lamb because it seemed to offer warmth and companionship for her child. It was the lamb that she thought about in the middle of the night, she told me, and gradually she was able to include her baby in her thoughts as well. It was the lamb that made the unthinkable thinkable.

There are whole studies done of symbols in our society, symbols that mean sex and power and religion, but hardly anyone mentions the little lambs out in our graveyards. They're missing something very powerful, I think. Those lambs stand for a whole lot more than we know, even those of us who see them all the time, or those of us who unhappily must choose them once in awhile. They are a sinking of the heart, a crying out, a sure knowledge that a young life didn't have a chance, a sign that we seek help beyond ourselves because death, especially the death of a child, is beyond us. Never underestimate a lamb.

As I stood before Vera's lamb, I asked the usual questions: What happened to her? What about her parents, how did they live through it? Were there other children? Does anyone remember her all these years later? And for once, I was able to get some answers. Her younger brother lives in Nanton still, and he remembers being told of a sister who had died of pneumonia. His mother didn't talk about it much, he remembers, but as he said, "People almost expected to lose some of their children somewhere along the line." Which is not to say that they didn't do everything possible to save them. They did, but there were no antibiotics, no modern hospitals and medicine. Half the time, there were no roads and no transportation to get a child to medical care even if it was available. Some of the time, there was no money. To be a child was to be an endangered species; to be a parent was a frightening prospect.

Calgary Union Cemetery has several sections set aside for the burial of babies. At first I thought this was done so that the babies might be company for one another, but I'm too woolly-headed for anything. There is a practical reason: baby sections are set aside because the lots can be smaller and therefore cheaper.

In one of the older baby sections is the Sketchley grave, topped by the ever-present lamb.

William George
Beloved Child of A.J. and M. Sketchley
Died Aug. 2, 1914, Aged 1 yr. 9 mos.
"Suffer little children to come unto me."

Unlike many of the smaller centres in Alberta, Calgary doesn't have a community history of its earliest citizens, so I had to go to the *Calgary Daily Herald* for clues about William George Sketchley's death. The obituary was there on August 3, 1914, one day after his death:

> The death occurred on Aug. 2 of William George Sketchley, aged 1 year, 6 mos., son of Mr. and Mrs. A.J. Sketchley, 1112 Bellevue Avenue, East Calgary. The funeral takes place from the family residence on Monday morning at 9 o'clock. Funeral services conducted by Rev. Mr. Gale. Interment takes place in Union Cemetery.

Not much information there as to the eternal Why? There was one article further on in the same paper about typhoid fever and how parents ought to boil all drinking water to be absolutely sure it was safe for their children. That could have been an answer. Later in the week, an article under the headline "Small Outbreak of Scarlet Fever Here" described how a local dairy had disinfected its plant after discovering that one of its workers was infected with scarlet fever. Assurances were given to the public that the problem had been dealt with, and the milk was now safe. Another possible reason why William George had died.

In fact, William George died of diphtheria, an infectious disease that affects the throat and eventually obstructs breathing. His sister, who still lives in the family home, remembered very well how devastated her mother was over the death of her son. "She was crazy about him," she said. She also remembered that a doctor had told her mother, "Some babies live and some babies die." It was cold comfort, but it was the truth in those days.

William George had the bad luck to die to begin with, but he also had the misfortune to die the same week as World War I started. As a news event, his death could not compete with the exciting possibility of war. The day that his quiet little obituary appeared on a back page, the front page trumpeted in six-inch high letters, "ALL WORLD AWAITS BRITAIN'S DECISION ON PEACE OR WAR," and story after story discussed the pros and cons of Britain's going to war against Germany. If Britain went to war, then Canada went to war.

Another headline proclaimed, "LOCAL MILITIA IS FULLY PREPARED TO PROTECT THE DOMINION, OVER 4,000 MEN CAN BE MOBILIZED AT ONCE, ALL READY TO DEFEND CANADA." It was apparently the most exciting thing that had happened in Canada and Calgary for a long time. The only note of caution was sounded in the editorial which began simply, "Armageddon has arrived."

And so it had. War was officially declared the next day, August 4, 1914, two days after William George fought his own small war — and lost.

~

A small fence is another sign of a young life finished too soon. Driving through the dry lands south of Medicine Hat one hot afternoon, I spied a graveyard behind St. Anthony's Roman Catholic Church. The church looked to be abandoned, but the graveyard was still in use. A few older graves were arranged in straggly lines at the back, and a brand new black granite marker at the front listed names of people buried in the cemetery but not marked.

As I walked through the brittle prairie grass to the old graves, I spied a combination wood and wire fence, and I knew right away it would contain the grave of a child. The fence was holding its own — still straight even though the wooden corner posts were bleached with age and worn right down to the grain — but the wooden cross inside the fence had fallen over. It was weathered like the fence posts, but the words carved there so many years ago were still visible: "Our Dear Randolph."

Once I had the name, I wondered about the rest. What happened to Randolph? Do any of his family ever come back and say his name, or am I the only one who has done so in a long time? Where do memories go anyway, after the people who can own them are no longer around?

~

Another fence worked its spell on me when I drove to Dunvegan, the broad valley alongside the Peace River just west of Fairview. The day I visited, the river was quiet, slower now that winter was near; the poplars and willows and wild rose bushes alongside its broad banks so brilliant they seemed plugged into something. But the maples were the best, strong and sure of themselves on a sun-dappled piece of the river bank. The occasional leaf drifted down to pile up with others on the ground beneath the trees, but it was a dignified process — these maples were the elders here; they would not be rushed into winter.

Back in the late 1800s, two missions were established in the Dunvegan area, one a Roman Catholic mission and the other Anglican. The Anglicans were second on the scene and never had a lot of success as far as saving souls was concerned, but Reverend Alfred Garrioch, the first minister at the mission, went out one day and planted some maple seeds on the river bank near the mission. I don't know if he even knew that the seeds had germinated before he had to leave for warmer climes, happier times, but germinate they did, and today they are a tourist attraction — the Maples Picnic site, under the bridge and just beyond the reconstructed Roman Catholic mission.

When the Garriochs left, they also left behind a small white picket

11

fence a few steps away from those maples, a boxlike enclosure just big enough to hold a child. The handwritten marker on the grave reads:

In Loving Memory of Caroline
Infant Daughter of Alfred and Agnes Garrioch
Who Died April 20, 1888, Aged 2 days
"Forever With the Lord"

It must have been hard to leave her behind when they had to move on. There was no one there to visit her or to put flowers on her grave now and then. They were leaving her in the wilderness, so Garrioch did the best he could. He built the picket fence to mark her place and keep the animals away. There was a practical purpose to those little fences as well as an aesthetic one, and sometimes the two purposes created a third entity: what modern artists would call conceptual art. That is, an art object that is greater than its pieces, greater than its form or the function that it serves. I'm over my head in discussions of art, but I know that Caroline's grave, standing alone in its own sunny wilderness alongside the river, represented more than a death. It looked like a poem, read like a painting, and as such was beautiful and awful at the same time.

Reverend Alfred Garrioch was so sincere, so valiant in the service of his Lord and the Anglican Church, but there must have been times while he was missionary at Dunvegan that he wondered why he was being punished. He knew that northern Alberta was no picnic — he had already served as a single man at Fort Chipewyan and Fort Vermilion — but there's nothing like a wife and babies to make life more difficult.

Garrioch met his future bride when he was in London, England, to oversee the publication of the New Testament in the alphabet which he had invented for the Beaver Indian language. The couple married early in 1886, and 100 days later, Mrs. Garrioch gazed upon her new home, the Anglican Mission house at Dunvegan, half a world away from London.

At Christmas time that year, Mrs. Garrioch gave birth to a baby boy. Although her husband wrote long and detailed reports to headquarters about his church work, he didn't even mention Frank's arrival. We don't know who attended the birth or how his wife managed her first labour. But he does give thanks in a later report for the fact that the baby Frank did not get measles or the whooping cough, even though the native woman who suckled him for awhile lived in a household full of the diseases.

Garrioch had a terrible time getting milk through the first winter of Frank's life. The cow that was supposed to be shipped to them in plenty of time for the baby never arrived, but he could still joke about it. In one of his books, he wrote:

> I received word that my cow had died on the way. But a little later reports reached me from disinterested sources leading me to believe that my cow was alive and flourishing at Sturgeon Lake.... When I came to study out the slow and costly process by which I could prove the identity of my cow, I decided to leave the matter alone, comforting myself with the reflection that if my cow was not dead she ought to be and that some day, perhaps before long, in the interests of justice, she would peacefully pass away.

The winter of 1887-88 was another long, hard one. The Garriochs operated a soup kitchen for as long as their supplies held out, but eventually they had to close down and try to find enough for themselves. By April, Rev. Garrioch's careful, stylish diary entries had become more frantic, more direct:

Tuesday, April 24: Snow storm. No school. Writing letters, studying, etc.

Wednesday, April 25: Birth of a daughter at 8 o'clock this morning. Mrs. Garrioch seems fairly comfortable. I write one hour after birth of baby. I am exceedingly thankful and I trust my gratitude will live as long as I do. "Bless the Lord O my Soul."

Thursday, April 26: Our dear little daughter passed away at 6 o'clock this evening. Its autograph text in Mrs. Garrioch's Book of Birthdays is "Blessed Be the Name of the Lord." And while our tears flow, we are endeavouring to be resigned. [The date that is on the grave now is out by six days. Perhaps recent maintenance mistook a six for a zero.]

Friday, April 27: Burial took place at 6:30 this evening, four men present. Mrs. Garrioch very weak and I am feeling quite anxious on her account.

Saturday, April 28: Mrs. Garrioch remaining weak and is suffering. Be merciful unto us O God.

Sunday, April 29: Only three present at service. Mrs. Garrioch easier.
Monday, April 30: Warm day. River opened opposite mission. No
     improvement in Mrs. Garrioch's health.

But by the next week, she was getting more rest, he reported, and by the
time he wrote his annual letter at Christmas that year, he was able to
report Caroline's death in a more philosophical framework:

> To everyone fit for heaven surely the death of a brother or sister
> saint should be only as the gentle moving of a treasure from earth
> where there is decay, to heaven where there is no corruption; the
> taking from here of what we cannot long hold or enjoy, and the
> placing of it where we may enjoy it forever. My good wife and I
> rejoice to be able to think thus as we look upon a little grave a
> few yards from the Mission house, where lies our infant daugh-
> ter born to us last April, and whose pure spirit returned to the
> God who gave it, after a short sojourn with us of a few hours.

Three years later, the Garriochs moved to the mission near Red River in
Manitoba. Caroline's small, fenced grave is all that now remains of their
habitation in the north, that and the maple trees.

$\sim$

Heart-shaped gravemarkers also warn of children ahead, like one in the
old Catholic Mission near Spirit River. There aren't many graves left in
the now-abandoned mission site, but one stands out with its heart shape
and its heartbreaking message, **"How much sorrow, How much joy, Is
buried with a darling boy? Edwin Lebeuf, aged four years."**

I haven't been able to find out anything about the Lebeuf family.
They are not included in the local history book and local historians are
equally baffled. All that is left of the Lebeufs — in that part of the world
anyway — is Edwin's marker, a small white heart that marks the time he
spent on this earth.

$\sim$

Sometimes there is no warning of a child's grave, no softening of the
edges of the truth. A plain grey concrete marker with the stark message
"Baby Born & Died April 23, 1912" stands in the Trochu Catholic Cemetery, and when I found it, I didn't expect to find out who it belonged to.

I didn't really need to know, since the whole sad story was told right there — in five words or less, the same story told over and over again in the bad old days. However, the probable identification of the anonymous baby jumped out at me as I read the story of Trochu.

The town of Trochu was the brainchild of three French immigrants: Armand Trochu for whom the town was named, Joseph Devilder, and Leon Eckenfelder. In 1904, they made plans to build a ranch, then a hotel, a store, and eventually a town. Everything was to be integrated; nothing was to be left to chance. But first the weather failed to cooperate, and then the CPR failed to come through. The winter of 1906-07 was so cold with so much snow that many of the cattle on the range died; the ranching operation took a huge blow. Then the railway bypassed the town. You just couldn't have a town without a railway in those days, so that was the end of the grand scheme. Armand Trochu and Joseph Devilder eventually went back to France.

Eckenfelder stayed on, and he and his wife, Valentine, had four children. It was in the listing of those four children in the local history book that I think I solved the mystery of the unidentified grave marker. The book tells us that Cecile was born in 1908 and George in 1910. Both lived to tell their own stories; however, the third child, Jeanne, was born in 1912 and lived only a day. Surely there wouldn't have been two babies in the Trochu area who were born and died on the same day in 1912, so I think the gravemarker must refer to her. The Eckenfelders had another child, Michel, born in 1913, who lived a week. The local history book doesn't reveal why the two youngest babies died. Maybe there was no doctor, likely there was no hospital, maybe the babies were premature.

How any children survived the dangers of life on the frontier is sometimes to be wondered at. Cecile Eckenfelder writes in the history book about the time they almost lost her brother George. They were travelling by horse and wagon on a steep hill in the Red Deer River Canyon when part of their wagon snapped.

Dad saved us by jumping out and putting a stone behind the wheels. He had to walk a half mile to the nearest house to get wire. Mother, who was very frightened of the horses, especially the big grey, had to hold them. George who was a baby just crawling kept going below the horses. But, everything ended happily.

Imagine having to stand still and hold the horses while your baby crawled around under their hooves! From then on, Cecile said, they got out of the wagon and walked up and down any steep banks.

When war was declared in 1914, Eckenfelder went back to France to join the French army. Peace brought him back to Trochu and eventually to Edmonton, but he never made it big, the way he and his original partners had intended. Trochu turned into a nice little town that in the last few years has gained a reputation for a certain tea room located in a certain picturesque old ranch house known as St. Ann's. And so the world turns.

~

Three identical markers, for Ruby Belle Myer, Eva Emerald Myer, and Alice Pearl Myer, side by side in the Vermilion Cemetery, brought out all the usual questions and then some. How could three little girls aged three, six, and eight have died within two days of one another? How could three little girls so carefully named for jewels have died before they had a chance to shine? Was it some terrible accident, or was it disease? I hadn't read of an epidemic occurring in 1907, but there could have been a local rush of diphtheria or typhoid. Or something.

The answer was not at all what I or probably anyone in Alberta would have expected. The Myer girls were killed by a tornado. The family lived on a farm in the Battle River Valley, and one hot summer afternoon, when the father and oldest son were in a distant field putting up hay, the sky turned a terrible shade of black and a fierce wind blew up in the valley. Mrs. Myer stayed in the house with the baby and the three little girls until it seemed as if the house would break into a thousand pieces, then she fled, carrying the baby and hurrying the little girls ahead of her. At that moment, the house did break into a thousand pieces. She was hurled to the ground, the baby pinned beneath her and safe because of that, but the girls were completely at the mercy of the storm. Ruby Belle and Eva Emerald were killed instantly when struck by flying logs from the house; Alice Pearl died from her injuries the next day.

They were buried beneath strong marble markers anchored to a concrete base, as if to stand firm in death, if not in life.

~

In Medicine Hat is another marker that commemorates children who were victims of unexpected weather: Arthur Moran Cochrane, aged fifteen years, and Harold Walton, aged ten. Their shared epitaph reads, **"They were lovely and pleasant in their lives; And in death they were not divided."**

One winter afternoon in 1891, Moran and Harold went riding together along Bull's Head Creek, a favourite trail near their homes. They only intended to be away for an hour or two, but in that time a terrible blizzard blew up, the kind that comes complete with snow so heavy you can't see and wind so fierce you can't breathe. The boys lost their way, and the horses couldn't help them. When they were found the next day, it looked as though Moran had tried to save the situation. His young companion was found wrapped in a horse blanket, sheltered by the saddle from his horse, as if Moran had said, "Wait here, I'll go get help." But he didn't make it back. Harold was covered with snow and frozen to death. Moran was found about a half mile away beside a haystack, his lifeless hands still holding onto his horse's harness.

For years their marker in the Kin Coulee graveyard was surrounded by an old bedstead which, along with the story of their death, turned them into something of a tourist attraction. In the last few years, however, the graveyard has been cleaned up by the local Rotary Club, and the boys are simply marked by a single pedestal tombstone.

~

For all her cruelty, nature can also be kind. When baby Ruth Van Der Velde died of whooping cough in the spring of 1922, she was buried in the Dalemead Cemetery. Writing in the local history book, her father remembered:

> On March 17, 1922, our youngest daughter Ruth was born. This was the year the whooping cough took so many babies and our little one was no exception. She passed away May 3. The funeral was held in the hall and the Dalemead children made wreaths of crocuses that grew so freely on the prairie. Prince and Dan, our best team, carried her to her last resting place.

Wreaths of crocuses — what could be more fitting for a child of the prairies?

~

I doubt if crocuses grow among the prairie grasses in the Granum Cemetery. It's just too windy, too inhospitable, for anything that frail. Even the tough old caragana in the hedge have to struggle to stay upright in the face of the winds that rule this barren piece of land. Still, it's never wise to judge a book by its cover. In that windswept, forlorn cemetery is one of the most moving gravestones I found in Alberta's graveyards.

It's the gravestone of young Johnny Maclean and at the base is a pair of boots and a cap, carefully carved into sandstone. I haven't been able to determine how or why young Johnny lost his life at eleven years of age in 1927, but I do know that it was his father who designed and made the original marker. After the funeral, he spied his son's boots and cap arranged neatly at the foot of his bed, just as Johnny had always left them, and he knew he had to work them into the design for his son's marker. They spoke to him then, and they speak to us still, telling those of us who find them that a boy lies here, a real boy who wore sturdy boots to walk the prairie grasses and a hat that he would surely have taken off when a lady entered the room. It's that kind of cap, and I'm guessing he was that kind of boy.

Johnny Maclean's dad, Duncan, came to the "Leavings" area near Claresholm from Scotland in 1904 and put his masonry skills to work right away by building a big stone house, the likes of which the log and frame houses in the district had seldom seen. In 1910, he opened a sandstone quarry at a site near Monarch on the Oldman River, and for the next four years, it was a thriving enterprise employing up to sixty people. Five more Maclean brothers and one sister joined Duncan in Canada; some joined the business. A townsite called Staunton developed around the quarry, but World War I changed everything. Many of the workers signed up. When they returned — if they returned — they found the quarry and town closed. There is nothing to mark Staunton now except some big holes in the river bank.

Duncan Maclean went into mixed farming and never went back to the masonry business, except when he had to make that tombstone for his boy. Fortunately the tombstone faces east, so the design elements are somewhat sheltered from the worst of the weather that comes from the west. The edges of the sandstone are softening, the words are getting hard to read, there's some rust and mold in the corners, but by and large, Duncan Maclean's dear Johnny is still well represented on this earth.

~

History books tell us about Ancel Maynard Bezanson's vision, his determination to tell the world about the Peace River country, his everlasting promotional schemes. But as far as I'm concerned, the most compelling story about Bezanson is the story of his baby son.

An adventurer and promoter, Bezanson walked, rode and paddled into the Peace River country in 1906 via the Athabasca Trail. He thought the country was grand, and the hilltop overlooking the Big Smoky, Wapiti, and Simonette Rivers seemed the ideal spot for a town. All he needed to make the town complete was a railway, and he was sure that would come. How could it not? His location had good water, good land, abundant timber, a gentle grade. It was the most logical site for miles around.

But railways didn't work by logic in those early days. The railway that finally rattled and rolled into the north was called the Edmonton, Dunvegan and British Columbia, the E.D. & B.C. for short. It went north through Athabasca to High Prairie and McLennan, where it branched off west to Grande Prairie and north to Peace River. It missed Bezanson's town by at least twenty miles. And it was no comfort to Bezanson that the E.D. & B.C. became known as the Exceedingly Dangerous and Badly Constructed Railway. As bad as it was, he wanted it. The town hung on for a few years, but eventually most people moved to Grande Prairie.

Before the dream died, however, Bezanson married Dorothy Robillard of Ottawa in 1908 and brought her to his beloved north country. They were joined in the summer months by Dorothy's sister Lois, and by all accounts, they had a fine time. Life was good, until Dorothy gave birth to their first child on Christmas Day, 1908. The baby was delivered safely, but even with her doctor father in attendance, Dorothy died.

It's the next part of the story that has become northern legend. Baby Frank could not survive without milk, the nearest cow was thirty-five miles away at the Clifford place, something had to be done. So in spite of terrible cold and a winter storm that limited visibility, Lois climbed into a sleigh, put the baby on her knee under so many blankets it was a wonder he could breathe, and set off for the Clifford place. Can you imagine heading out into a winter storm with a newborn baby to find milk and help? I still wonder why they didn't bring the milk to the baby. I also wonder why they hadn't thought about the possible need for a cow before the birth took place. Still, it's not fair of me to make judgments from this side of the story. Lois did manage the incredible trip.

Two years later, Bezanson and Lois were married. Their first children were twin girls, stillborn. They were buried behind the house that was still waiting for the rest of the town to arrive. A year later, Jim was born. Both he and Frank lived to tell the tale.

Pioneer women are not often recognized for their part in building the west, but on the edge of the river bank where Bezanson built the first house in his town-that-couldn't-miss, there is a handsome stone cairn in honour of "The Pioneer Women — Lois and Dorothy Robillard-Bezanson." The sculpted bronze plaque depicts a woman holding a baby in her arms, a sleigh and horse behind her. It is a tribute to Lois's incredible ride through the winter storm with her newborn nephew in her arms; it's a tribute to the women who all too often died in childbirth; it says that it took women as well as men to build this new world.

≈

In the summer, the Lac La Biche Mission Cemetery is a sweet tangle of grasses, wild roses, peavine, wild strawberries, and goldenrod. The old gravemarkers look right at home, edges softened and held up by the growth around them, the newer ones still a bit self-conscious.

Across the road, the tourists troop in and out of the newly restored mission buildings, diligently registering the fact that this remote mission was established in 1855 and wasn't all that remote, considering that most trans-Canada transportation in those days took place on northern rivers. Lac La Biche was right in the middle of the action then, which is why W.E. Traill was pleased to be posted there in 1874. He was to be head of the Hudson's Bay Company trading post, a move that would be good for his career, he hoped, but one that proved to be a disaster in other ways.

First, his daughter Molly died of whooping cough on the journey to Lac La Biche. She was buried in Prince Albert. A few years later, two other children died during an outbreak of scarlet fever in the community. It was their gravemarker that caught my attention in the mission cemetery, one of the oldest gravemarkers I found in Alberta. It's a small white marble headstone that explains that Catharine Parr and Henry, eldest daughter and infant son of W.E. and H. Traill, died in December 1879, aged respectively seventeen years and thirteen months.

The final lines say, **"They cannot come to us but we may go to them."**

How did they do it, I wondered, as I stood before the little marble marker, its message still heartbreakingly clear so many years later. How did they accept such tragedy?

But, of course, they didn't. They were just as heartbroken as modern parents would be. They simply had no defense against the diseases and accidents that took their children. As a result, they learned to be stoic, and they relied on their faith. This is what W.E. Traill wrote to his mother about the death of his children.

> I trust that I am fully resigned to the Divine will, and I know that my darlings are infinitely happier where they are, but still the flesh is weak and the heart yearns with an unspeakable longing after the dear absent ones. Of the five children born to us, we have only two left now; no wonder then if at times we feel our loss very keenly.

No wonder, indeed. Incidentally, W. E. Traill was the son of the well-known author, Catharine Parr Traill, who wrote, among other things, a book called *The Backwoods of Canada*. And that's not the end of the interesting ripples of this story. W.E. Traill's grandson, Pat McCloy, was the first librarian at the Glenbow in Calgary. "In my nearly seventeen years there," he wrote to me, "I developed a library in which I take great pride." In the collection he organized are copies of the correspondence between his grandfather and great-grandmother, one of the ways we can read our history now.

One of the other ways is to stand before a lonesome grave.

~

THE LAST WORD: This epitaph appears on the grave of Madge MacConnal, 1903-16, in the Pine Lake Anglican Church Cemetery east of Red Deer.

But O for the touch of a vanished hand
And the sound of a voice that is still.

Stories of Love

In Loving Memory of Emily
The Loved Wife of Sydney Charles Yeoman
Who died May 15, 1932, aged 55 years.
"Oh, How I Miss You
Dear Old Pal of Mine"

...epitaph in the Jasper Cemetery

"How do I love thee? Let me count the ways." So wrote Elizabeth Barrett Browning in one of the most famous love poems ever. If you choose to take her advice and go in search of loving words between men and women, husbands and wives, in Alberta graveyards, let me warn you — they are few and far between. We write beautiful, heartbreaking inscriptions on the graves of our children and our parents, but our tongues are tied when it comes to declarations of love between men and women. If there is any such talk, it's generally the women who choose the loving words and the men who get them on their gravemarkers. Thus, men more often than women are immortalized by expressions such as "**Dearly Beloved**" or "**Sadly Missed**" or "**My Darling Farewell**," perhaps because women often survive their male partners and thus are around to choose the words for the marker. Also, women are expected to get mushy now and then; it goes with the territory.

But men are expected to be strong and matter-of-fact, so they pick out the stuff of which true romance is made out here in the wild west. Theirs are the extravagant tributes like "**Mother**" for the grave of the little woman. Sometimes they add "**Rest in Peace**," which is a nice idea but somehow seems a bit inadequate after a shared lifetime. To be fair, it is often the children of the family selecting the final words, so they naturally tend toward "**Mother**." But that still doesn't completely explain the scarcity of romance in the graveyard.

However and however, there are lovely exceptions. In the Medicine Hat graveyard is a tall pedestal of white marble topped with the universal symbol of the mourning mother. The inscription reads:

Janet Johnston
The wife of Dan McLain
Born Jan. 11, 1885, Died April 28, 1918.
"One of the Best Women That Ever Lived"

High praise indeed — if only Dan McLain had been able to go the whole way and pronounce his wife "The Best!" The inscription on the other side of the pedestal is more straightforward: **In Memory of Dan McLain, Born Jan. 11, 1853, Died April 17, 1929.**

The museum in Medicine Hat couldn't find any record of the romantic Mr. McLain until they realized that his name was also spelled McLean. It often happens in graveyard research that names and dates are inaccurate, even though they're recorded in stone. Dan McLean, it was discovered, had come to Medicine Hat from Scotland and worked on the CPR until he bought land further south. There he raised cattle and sheep, but in 1917, he gave up on farming and moved back to the city. A year later, his wife died, and he marked her with the loving words that still speak to us.

∼

The Coleman Cemetery in the Crowsnest Pass contains another lovely tribute to a wife. It's written in memory of the beloved wife of John Johnston, Annie, who was born on May 20, 1866, and died on March 25, 1924.

If I had the wings of morning, love
I would soon fly up to thee
For my heart is a'breaking, love
Since I had to part from thee.

Even though local historians checked all possible spellings, they couldn't determine the identity of John and Annie Johnston. A John Johnston served as mayor of Coleman in the 1920s and was very active in the life of the community, but it was not the same John Johnston who wrote poetry on his wife's grave.

∼

The Athabasca graveyard in northern Alberta also contains poetry dedicated to the memory of a beloved companion — Hilda Amy, wife of Edgar Mellor, who died April 11, 1913, aged twenty-six.

Whatever way my days decline
I felt and feel tho' left alone
Her being working in mine own
The footsteps of her life in mine.

It almost begins to look like a plot, as if poetry of any sort means immediate expulsion from community memory, but Athabasca historians can't identify this poet in their midst either. All they could find was an obituary of another Mellor, Arthur Howard Llewellyn, who died in Victoria in 1950. A member of the RCMP, he was transferred to the Athabasca area in 1908 and remained there for awhile, the obituary says. It could be that this Mellor was a brother or relative living with him or near him in 1913 when the death occurred. Or it could be no connection at all.

$\approx$

The message on the Christie grave in the Edmonton Cemetery is also unabashedly sweet, but this time its history is known. Almost lost in the grass and overwhelmed by the glory of the markers around it, it's a small marble marker in memory of Sarah, wife of C.D. Christie, who died May 18, 1906, aged thirty-eight years, two months, eight days.

Art thou weary? art thou languid?
Art thou sore distressed?
Come to Me, saith one, and
comming be at rest.
Erected by her sorrowing husband, Sept. 26, 1908.

Sarah Christie was the wife of Charles Christie, a well-known Hudson's Bay employee at McKenzie River, a connection which rated her a fairly prominent obituary. She came into Edmonton from McKenzie River two weeks before her death for "medical treatment," the obituary explained, and her funeral took place from the residence of Dr. McKay in Edmonton. Charles Christie didn't get around to having the marker erected until two years after Sarah's death, but speaking as one who seeks out loving messages, I believe it was worth the wait.

$\approx$

Finally, in the interests of fair play and equal rights, the following is a piece of poetry written in memory of a husband. I found it in the Nanton graveyard, a piece of land that the prairie has just barely surrendered. It's a valiant little graveyard, standing up tall and straight on a hillside south of town, but nature can't resist it. The native grasses nibble at the edges, the wind brings tumbleweed to lodge beside the gravemarkers, snow drifts at will in the winter. Like all graveyards, though, it has its lovely moments. This is what it says on the monument of William H. Baker, who died on August 21, 1920, aged thirty-four years, four months.

Oh I think of you, dear husband
And my heart is sore with pain
And the world would be a heaven
Could I hear your voice again.
I, who loved you, sadly miss you
As it dawns another year
In the lonely hours of thinking
Thoughts of you are ever near.

Again, there is no information on this Baker family in local history. Speak of love in Alberta graveyards and you'll be stricken from the record, or so it would appear!

That loving messages are the exception and not the rule in our grave-yards is often explained away by money. People just didn't have the money in Alberta's early days, or so the story goes. But the fact is that words on a gravemarker did not normally cost extra; nor do they now. The marker and installation came as a package with words included, as many as you liked. There would be additional charges for words added to an existing gravemarker, but generally speaking, the words ordered up at the time of purchase were not limited by a charge per word or per character. So there could have been more loving messages in our graveyards, and their absence points more to our regional character than to empty pockets

Cowboys may cry, but for whatever reasons, we don't do it in public.

~

One summer afternoon, I met a sweet, white-haired woman in the Medi-cine Hat Cemetery who proceeded to talk my leg off, telling me in the course of her story that she would not be buried with the nice old man who was waiting patiently for her in the nearby car. It's like this, you see. He has been married before and there is a place waiting for him beside his first wife because his first wife had given him a son and she (my little old lady) has not and the son made all the difference but my little old lady has never been married before so there is no one waiting for her so she will just be cremated and scattered on her parents' graves even though that's not what she really wants because she loves Ernie dearly but that's how it is. (And that's how she talked, without punctuation.) "It's too bad," she said, "I'd like to be with him, we've been through a lot, but that's how it is." Then she took her leave, explaining as she drove away that they had more friends to visit — in the graveyard, that is. I think of her when I see a double gravemarker with one side blank and expectant. She has decided not to do that to her husband and his family. She will go it alone, but I hope someone puts some loving words over her when the time comes.

My little old lady had put her finger on a very sticky problem: when one spouse dies and the remaining spouse remarries, who is buried with whom? Funeral directors tell me it's a situation that causes all kinds of bitterness and pain, especially if a double header — that is, a headstone with space for two names — is ordered after the death of one spouse. If it should happen that the remaining spouse chooses to be buried with someone else, then that bare spot on the marker becomes an ever-present reminder that dad didn't love mom enough to be buried with her, or mom left poor old dad out here alone. There are charges of betrayal and hurt feelings all round. Get individual markers, the funeral industry advises, and discuss all eventualities with family members before it's too late.

$\sim$

If sticky situations occur in the graveyard when a man or woman remarries, what happens in a graveyard when a man has had two or more wives at the same time? That's the question that took me to the Cardston Cemetery, where I thought I might find graves from earlier days when Mormons still practiced polygamy. Surely that practice would lead to some interesting combinations in the graveyard, I thought, and some delicate wording on the epitaphs. However, my search was in vain. I couldn't find any examples of multiple marriages in the graveyard. I found lots of similar last names which might have signalled more than one family per father — Leavitt, for example — but I didn't find a gravemarker with one husband, three wives, that sort of thing. Nothing out of the ordinary.

Cardston is named for Charles Ora Card, who did have more than one wife at a time. He had four, to be exact, and it was because of his multiple wives that he came to Canada in the first place. The United States passed a law outlawing polygamy in 1882, and as a result, Mormon men who chose to obey their church rather than the state were harassed, fined, imprisoned, denied the vote, denied the right to hold public office, generally hounded on all sides. Some went into hiding, some moved their several families around to different states or to Mexico, and some, like Card, looked north to Canada.

Thus it was that Card left his home in Utah in the spring of 1887, under the cover of darkness and a disguise, to move to Canada. Like the underground railway in eastern Canada that helped Black Americans escape the States, Card and the eight other men in the party depended on sympathetic spotters along the way to warn them of any possible trouble. The spotters told them which roads were safe, which stopping places could be trusted. It's no wonder that as soon as they were safely into Canada, Card and his companions gave three cheers "for our liberty as exiles for our religion."

Zina Card followed in a covered wagon several weeks later. She was Card's second wife and the only one to come to Canada. The daughter of Mormon leader Brigham Young, she was a chip off the old block by all accounts, a strong, independent woman who encouraged and sometimes financed a number of local businesses, among them a general store, flour mill, cheese factory, and sawmill. In the meantime, her husband brought more and more Mormon settlers to the area to work on irrigation projects, a win/win situation for both the Mormons and the North Western Coal and Navigation Company. The Mormon men wanted land and a refuge from the U.S. government; the coal company wanted to sell land and coal and irrigation. Both got their wishes.

The Mormon church eventually followed the government lead and suspended its practice of polygamy. Consequently, younger Mormon settlers in Alberta never suffered the same degree of discrimination that their elders had. They never took more than one wife. Some of the older settlers continued to support two or three families, but the practice died out with that generation, which is why there are no examples of multiple marriages in the Cardston Cemetery.

The Cards returned to the United States in the early 1900s — Charles to Logan, where he lived with his fourth wife until his death in 1906, and Zina to Salt Lake City, where she died in 1931. They were buried separately.

~

Pat Burns must have marvelled at the Mormon men with their multiple wives. He couldn't even get along with one. Burns is the kind of hero we like out here in the West. He made his money by selling good Alberta beef, he gave his money away to good Alberta causes like the Calgary Stampede, and he never let himself get proud. Even though he was named a Senator a few years before his death — and that was in the days when to be a senator was an honour — he still remained a humble rancher and businessman, the little guy who made good.

Even his gravemarker carries on the less-rather-than-more tradition established during his lifetime. It's fairly grand, in a prime spot overlooking the city in Calgary's St. Mary's graveyard, but it doesn't scream money. The attached bronze plaque says simply, **"Senator Patrick Burns, July 6, 1856-February 24, 1937, Pioneer, Rancher, Meat Packer, A Builder of the West."**

But it was that same understated gravemarker that led me down a garden path that I never knew existed. You see, Mrs. Burns is not buried there with him as one might expect. There is a son who died five months before his dad. But there's no mom in the equation. Where did she end up, I wondered? And why don't we hear anything about her? Ask an innocent question about what you find (or don't find) in the graveyard, and you may learn more than you bargained for. In this case, it turned out to be a love story that did not end happily ever after.

I began my quest for information at the Glenbow Archives in Calgary, where I innocently asked for the newspaper clipping file on Mrs. Burns. After all, there are books and files and boxes of stuff about Burns and his businesses; surely there would be a word or two about the missus. But there was no file on her at all. Nothing about her in her husband's file either. I checked the photograph archives next. Nothing. One or two photos of the son and rafts of pictures about the businesses, but nothing about Mrs. Burns.

Next I checked out Grant MacEwan's biography on Pat Burns. Again, more information than I ever wanted to know about business mergers and ranches and meat-packing plants, but not a whisper of romance until finally, well into the book, Grant MacEwan tells us how Pat Burns saw one Eileen Ellis coming down a staircase in a Penticton hotel. That's the one I'll marry, he told a companion. She was the daughter of the Ellis family, well-known ranchers of the Okanagan Valley, and Burns did indeed marry her, four years later in London, England. He brought her home to the biggest house in Calgary, a sandstone castle that he had built for her, and that should have been the beginning of good times.

It seems that isn't quite how it worked out; not that Grant MacEwan, ever the gentleman, would admit as much in the biography. He tells us a son, Patrick Michael, was born in 1906. Mrs. Burns moved away, and some time later, she died of stomach cancer in Vancouver.

I checked the *Calgary Herald* of the week of her death, expecting to find a lengthy obituary and the answers to some of my questions. But other than a terse, three-line announcement of her death, there was no further word about Mrs. Burns. No obituary at all. It was all very mysterious. What had this woman done that she was erased so completely from Calgary society?

From reading between the lines and talking to some old-timers, I found out that Mrs. Burns was not happy in her marriage and eventually left her husband. There are even hints of a love affair with another man that so hurt the pride of a certain stubborn Irishman that he never mentioned her name again. Neither did the community. There was, it seems, a gentleman's agreement. Mrs. Burns disappeared from Calgary records with barely a ripple. But I wanted to end the story. Where was she buried? And what did it say on her gravemarker? There was never a divorce, of course: Pat Burns was Catholic; Eileen Burns was a staunch Anglican. Divorce just wasn't an option in those days.

I began the search for her gravemarker in Vancouver. No luck. Friends checked out graveyards in the Okanagan area on the supposition that she might be buried with other members of the Ellis family. Again, no luck, but in the course of that search, someone mentioned the Ross Bay Cemetery in Victoria, B.C. Another search, this time successful. Mrs. Burns is buried in the Ellis family plot in the old Victoria Cemetery. Her marker is a simple grey granite cross that reads, **"In Loving Memory of Eileen Louisa, Wife of Patrick Burns, Sept. 7, 1923, Aged 50 years."** Far over the mountains lie her husband and her only son.

~

The story of Father Cesaire Mariman O.M.I. is another story of love, only this love involves the love of God and the love shared by a congregation and their priest.

When I started my graveyard research, I had no idea how many shrines we have in Alberta, all of them modelled after the famous Lourdes in France, which millions of worshippers visit every year in hopes of a physical or spiritual cure. There's a famous church there and sacred waters, but the most important feature of Lourdes is the rock grotto into which is built a niche containing a statue of the Virgin Mary. It was at this site that a fourteen-year-old peasant girl named Bernadette Soubirous saw the Virgin Mary in a total of eighteen visions and promised to build a shrine on the spot someday. She joined a religious order, fulfilled her promise, and became Saint Bernadette in 1933.

Of the Lourdes look-alikes in Alberta, the most original, the one with the best story, has to be the Eleske Shrine on the Beaver Indian reservation in northern Alberta, about halfway between High Level and Fort Vermilion. I had been told that the Eleske graveyard had some of the best examples of "spirit houses" in the province, and that turned out to be true. Spirit houses are little wooden frame structures built over individual graves. Some in this graveyard are painted white; some are so old that the wood is bleached white; some have scallops along the roof line; some have an additional wooden fence around them; all have wooden crosses at the peak of the roof. They're really very lovely, especially in the summertime when they're set against the surrounding green grass and trees.

Not everyone agrees on the definition of "spirit house." Our guide, a thoroughly modern young native woman named Rose, said that spirit house was just a name with very little significance anymore. "Hardly anyone builds a spirit house anymore," she explained. But others hold to the old tradition that the spirit house shelters the spirits of the dead person until they are ready to join the ancestors. Others who take a more pragmatic approach to these things say simply that spirit houses were originally built to keep the dogs from digging up the bones, which is why they're also known as "dog houses."

Whatever the origin, the spirit houses were lovely, a welcome treat from all the generic graveyards in our midst, but the shrine was the biggest surprise. It's built into the river bank below the graveyard, and it has all the required elements: a rock wall, niches that contain religious statues, an altar, the Stations of the Cross, and confessional booths. It was all quite remarkable.

As I discovered, there are two stories about the building of the shrine: a tale on the tall side that gets taller all the time and the real story recounted by Father Mariman before he died. Mind you, the real story is almost as remarkable as the legend that's growing.

Legend has it that a priest left the North to visit his home order in France. When it was time to return, the order gave him a beautiful statue of the Virgin Mary as a gift for his people in North America. On the way home, the priest was shipwrecked off Mexico. The only thing he was able to save was the statue. He tucked the statue under his arm, then hitchhiked, walked, talked, and prayed his way from Mexico to northern Alberta. He did it all without any money, the statue his only resource.

His parishioners were so impressed with the power of the statue that they decided to build a shrine in her honour. And that's how the Eleske Shrine came about — only it wasn't that way at all.

Father Mariman says in his written account that it was really his predecessor Rev. Father Habay who got the whole thing started in 1935, when a small church was built on the reservation. Because Father Habay was originally from near Lourdes area, and because Sister Bernadette from the same region had just been made Saint Bernadette, he decided to name her as patron saint of the new congregation.

Certainly the new congregation needed a patron saint. They were poor, and many of them suffered from tuberculosis. They might have been able to overcome poverty, but they couldn't overcome tuberculosis. By the time Father Mariman arrived on the scene, the disease had "mowed" entire families, as he put it. "It left me no hope to save from complete extinction the Beaver Indian tribe of the north Vermilion area, except if God would intervene directly or indirectly." He thought of Lourdes and the cures that were accomplished there by faith in God, and he decided that Eleske needed to go one step further. They had selected St. Bernadette as patron saint. Why not make a shrine like hers as well? As Father Mariman said, "Why could the Indians not experience the same supernatural intervention right here at an imitation grotto, if it would please God to show His Almighty power here?"

His superior Bishop Routhier OMI agreed to the idea with one "irksome condition," according to Father Mariman, that being that the congregation had to pay for the shrine entirely by themselves. There would be no help from headquarters. If the shrine were to perform miracles once built, some miracles had to happen during the building process as well, the Bishop decreed.

Now, it's one thing to get physical labour for free and building materials like rocks from the nearby Boyer River — the parishioners willingly hauled and dug and prepared the site for the shrine — but it's quite another to get the cement to hold the rocks in place. Cement requires money.

It was the story of the loaves and fishes all over again. A contractor from High Level donated some leftover supplies of cement, as did the hospital in Fort Vermilion. Unfortunately the cement was old and hardpacked, so it had to be pulverized into granular form again. That's where Father Mariman's special skills came into play. He hadn't grown up in windmill country in Belgium for nothing. He rigged up a windmill onto an old grain crusher, hung cement sacks on the arms to catch the wind and set the whole contraption on a wagon. "Then the good God sent a strong wind to make it turn in full speed," he recounted later. Soon the windmill powered the oat crusher, which in turn crushed the hard cement, which held the rocks together to build the shrine.

That accomplished, the parishioners realized they would need some lumber to reinforce the archway over the altar. There was still no money, but one of Father Mariman's Ukrainian friends agreed to hold a bingo in his own home, sell his wife's cooking, and donate the proceeds to the shrine. That was a great idea, except that everyone on or near the reserve was about as poor as the church was. They netted only $18, an amount they feared would fill the good father with despair. Instead, it filled him with great joy. He saw the number eighteen as a sign that God would see this project through, no matter what. After all, hadn't Saint Bernadette seen the Virgin Mary eighteen times?

And so he soldiered on, getting enough money but never too much to pay for the expenses of the shrine as it grew on the bank of the Boyer. The first pilgrimage was held in the fall of 1945, when it was still mostly a "concept" in Father Mariman's mind. The original shrine was finished in 1954, then renovated again in 1979. A pilgrimage is held every year.

And yes, it did bring better luck and better health to the Eleske region. "As far as I know," Father Mariman wrote, "all were blessed for their generosity in enjoying better health, better crops, etc..... those who seemed to love God with absolutely pure intentions were paid back for the work of their hands and the generosity of their prayers and sacrifices by much better blessings than any material ones."

And speaking of love, when Father Mariman died in 1989, his parishioners wrote on his black granite gravemarker, **"Our beloved priest who served the people of this area for over 50 years."**

~

The single most popular epitaph in Alberta graveyards is **Ever Loved, Ever Remembered**, which seems to contradict my theory that westerners have a hard time saying love in our graveyards, unless we're speaking of a priest perhaps or a mother. In fact, "Ever Loved, Ever Remembered" is quintessentially us. It includes the two emotions most important during mourning — love and remembering — but it doesn't get mushy. That's the important consideration: it allows us to hint at our feelings without actually naming them.

The other reason why this particular epitaph appears everywhere in our graveyards is Charlie MacLean. He was the manager of MacLean Granite in central Alberta for years, and it was his favourite. He urged it upon his customers, they in turn urged it upon others, and soon it was everywhere. Never let it be said that one person can't make a difference!

Other popular epitaphs that say less rather than more in our graveyards are: **"Rest In Peace," "Gone But Not Forgotten," "Life's Work Well Done," "At Rest**," and **"The Reward of Toil Is Rest."** But don't believe everything that you see. Albertans may seem stoic from the epitaphs found on our graves, but under all that bluff beats many a heartfelt emotion. That we have graveyards at all is a sign of love or community respect or tradition — call it what you will. If we were as tough as we like to pretend, we wouldn't bother with special places for the deceased, we wouldn't pay our taxes to have city or municipal governments maintain cemeteries, and if we lived in a rural area, we sure wouldn't attend "cemetery clean-up days," the better to break our backs pulling weeds and mowing grass. But we continue to do these things. As a matter of fact, we get right choked up if they're not done well.

We also buy gravemarkers for our family and community members. We may not say very much on them, but that piece of marble or granite is an emotional response to death. It is the triumph of passion over reason, and it sometimes surprises us with the feelings that come with it. I know all the modern arguments that soon there won't be enough room to bury us all and that cremation is the only responsible and sensible option left. That may be true, but I think there is some need in us to express love in more concrete ways — sometimes literally — and to carve our expressions of love into stone.

And then there is the love that was demonstrated by a frail old woman I met in the graveyard one day. She looked so upset that I asked her what the trouble was.

"It's the GST," she told me.

Complaining about the newly imposed Goods and Services Tax was nothing new right then; everyone was unhappy about it in one way or another. Somehow the graveyard didn't seem to be the most appropriate place to be discussing it. Then she explained that the GST even applied to the artificial flowers she bought for her husband's grave. That was going too far. She nodded toward her husband's grave. "He's been dead for fifteen years," she said. "I come every week. In the summer, I bring flowers from the garden but in the winter, I got to buy them, and they charge GST. It's not right."

She had arthritis, she could barely bend over, her feet hurt, but what really made her mad was a government, a society, that didn't understand what she had to do. But will she stop coming to the graveyard? No, never, she told me. "It wouldn't be right if I didn't come."

∽

THE LAST WORD: Speaking of love, this beautiful epitaph appears in the Olds Cemetery on the grave of Aileen Duff, 1906-30, beloved wife of S. H. Holloway. It's a version of the poem that Mark Twain wrote for his young daughter's grave.

Warm southern sun, shine kindly here
Warm southern winds, blow softly here
Green sod above, lie light, lie light,
Good night, good night.

Hillside Cemetery, Medicine Hat

Stories Told Well and Truly

In Memory of
Captain Sir Cecil Edward Denny BT
Sixth Baronet of Tralee Castle, Ireland
Born in Hampshire, England, 14th Dec. 1850
Died in Edmonton, Alberta, 24th August, 1928
Crossed the plains in 1874 as Inspector in
The original North West Mounted Police
Co. Founder of Forts Macleod and Calgary
Honorary Chieftain in Blackfoot Nation
Indian Agent, Government Archivist
Explorer, Pioneer, Adventurer & Author
He knew not fear. A born optimist

...epitaph on Cecil Denny grave in Union Cemetery, Calgary

When I found the Cecil Denny gravemarker, all I could say was, Wow! It told the story of one man's life so completely that I couldn't help but know a great deal about Captain Denny after reading the words on his grave. But besides the personal story, his gravemarker told the story of the West. It was all there — immigration and the North West Mounted Police and settlement and displacement, a textbook written in stone.

I was alone in the huge cemetery that day, except for the maintenance people, and I wondered why. Why aren't history classes out here? Why aren't groups of tourists trailing past? Cecil Denny's gravemarker by itself touches upon the major themes of western settlement, and because it belongs to a real person, students and others couldn't conclude that we don't have history in this part of the world, and even if we do, it's boring. No way. Cecil Denny is real, history is real.

In 1874, Cecil Denny was a young man looking for a bit of adventure. When he heard that the Canadian government was recruiting men to form a police force in western Canada, he joined up. He knew beans about the West; he knew even less about Indians and the illegal liquor trade; he just knew the trip across the Canadian prairies sounded like the adventure he was looking for. And it was, especially when the food ran out, and storms killed the horses, and travel was so hard as to be almost impossible. Other than that, it was a great adventure for the 274 men who left Manitoba one sunny July day. And just as advertised, they set about doing police work as soon as they unpacked their bags at Fort Macleod five months later.

Everything those first NWMP members did, they had to do by the seat of their pants, and for the first few years they managed quite nicely, establishing good relations with the Indians. By the time Treaty #7 was signed in 1877, however, relations between the Indians and representatives of the government in Ottawa had deteriorated. The NWMP managed to keep the lid on the situation; they were on the spot and more sympathetic to the Indian cause. Then a Department of Indian Affairs was created, and Indian agents were hired. That didn't work nearly so well because decisions were made in Ottawa and imposed from the outside.

Cecil Denny could see the problems of this new system so he decided to become an Indian agent, thinking he could continue to champion the Indian cause from within the bureaucracy. That worked for a while. He had some 7,000 Indians under his wing in Treaty #7, with more and more responsibilities coming his way all the time, until the Ottawa government cut back on his staff and told him to cut back on rations to the Indians as well. He was so disgusted that he resigned forthwith.

That was in 1884. A year later, he was asked to come back and appease the Indians of southern Alberta, just in case they might decide to join Louis Riel and the Metis in the North West Rebellion. One of the first things he did was increase the rations of meat and flour to the Indians. They might not be so interested in fighting if they weren't hungry, he felt.

His life continued to mirror history. He decided to try homesteading for awhile. Why not? Everyone else was. Then, like a lot of other homesteaders, he discovered homesteading didn't make much money, so he went exploring, then joined a survey crew, then tried his hand at writing.

In 1922, when his half-brother died in England, he succeeded to his title as Baronet of Tralee in Ireland, not that it made much of a difference to his life. He never got much money from it; he certainly never inhabited a castle or rubbed shoulders with royalty. In fact, that same year, he quietly moved to Edmonton and became the official historian and archivist for the province of Alberta.

After his death in Edmonton in 1928, Calgary didn't even mention his passing in the daily newspaper. A memorial service was held in Edmonton, and his body was quietly buried in Calgary, but it was ten years before Calgary remembered its manners and did the right thing by Sir Cecil Denny. On June 13, 1938, a fairly grand ceremony was held at Union Cemetery to unveil the marker that now stands at the head of his grave. The mayor was there, along with the bishop and representatives of different branches of the RCMP and armed forces. The actual unveiling was done by Fred Bagley, who had been the boy trumpeter on that historic march across the plains by the original members of the NWMP. He didn't play "The Last Post" as he had done for his fallen comrades on the trail so many years earlier. That honour fell to the trumpeters from Lord Strathcona's Horse, and you could hear their tribute all over the growing and booming city where once, as Denny had written in his early journal, "of man we saw at first no sign." Who could have predicted so many changes in one lifetime?

≈

Norman Luxton's gravemarker in the Banff Cemetery is, for my money, the next best gravemarker in Alberta as far as story telling is concerned. It commemorates **"Norman Kenny Luxton, 1874-1962, Sailed Pacific Ocean from Vancouver to New Zealand in Thirty Foot Dugout 'Tilikum' 1902. And his wife Georgia Elizabeth, 1870- 1965, Born Fort Victoria North (Pakan), First white child born in Alberta."** Who could possibly look at those words without wondering how the heck a guy from a dozy little mountain town like Banff ever got himself on an Indian dugout crossing the Pacific Ocean? If he had climbed the world's highest mountain it wouldn't be so surprising. But to tackle an ocean...now that's a story.

Norman Luxton came west as a seventeen-year-old, planning to get rich in the Cariboo gold fields of British Columbia. When that didn't work, he decided to become a newspaperman in Calgary. When that didn't work, at least not for Luxton, he sailed half-way around the world in a dinky little boat that didn't look sturdy enough to go cruising down the river on a Sunday afternoon.

It all began in a Vancouver bar where Luxton was having a beer with an old sailor named John Voss. They got talking about boats and oceans and winds and such. Voss revealed that he knew where he could get a thirty-foot cedar dugout, the real thing used by West Coast Indians. It needed work, but he figured it could be rigged up to sail two men strong and true around the world. No sweat. Would young Luxton like to join him? In addition, would young Luxton like to pay for the repairs and finance the trip?

Young Luxton's mother had a fit. She sent Norman's older brother out to the coast to dissuade him from such a foolhardy notion, but Norman had made up his mind. It would be a grand adventure. He would pay to have the boat repaired and outfitted for their ocean voyage, and then he could sell the story of the voyage to papers around the world. What a great way to break into the big time of journalism. Besides, Voss seemed to know everything there was to know about boats and navigation. He'd been on the water ever since he was a kid in Denmark. What could go wrong?

Most everything, as it turned out. The pair set sail on the newly renovated Tilikum at the beginning of June, 1901. Tilikum means "friend" in the Chinook language, but the name soon proved inappropriate. Luxton and Voss grew to dislike one another thoroughly, and by the time they got to their first stop in the South Seas two months later, they were speaking only when spoken to. Together they had faced storms, constant bailing, the loss of their drinking water, a shortage of food, an abundance of sharks and whales, but these experiences had not united them in any way. Thus, when a chieftain on one of the first South Sea Islands offered Luxton all the food he could eat plus one of his daughters — a number one princess, he was told — Luxton was tempted to accept, not for the princess, he made clear later, but for the chance to be away from Voss.

Between the island of Samoa and Fiji, the Tilikum smashed onto a coral reef, and Luxton, who was pitched out of the boat, had to make a choice between the calmer shark-infested waters or the pounding waters over the reef. He chose the reef, but by daybreak he was more or less dead. When he came to, he was sure that Voss was measuring him for a grave in the sand. The two men reached the island of Suva on October

17, 1901, some four and one-half months after leaving Victoria, but it was to be the end of the voyage for the battered Luxton. A doctor on Suva told him that continuing the voyage would be the same as committing suicide.

Voss sailed on with various other sailing partners, one of whom died at sea — Luxton was convinced there was foul play, but nothing could ever be proven — and eventually reached England, where he enjoyed fame and glory for a year or two. He published a book called *The Venturesome Voyages of Captain Voss*, but as the accomplishment faded from public interest, so did the boat and the boatman. The Tilikum was discovered years later in a marine graveyard beside the Thames, where it would be still if some Canadian historians hadn't reclaimed it and found a home for it at the Maritime Museum in Victoria.

When Norman Luxton got back to Canada, his friends took one look at him and prescribed Banff. He was some forty pounds underweight, beaten up and sobered by his near brushes with death. He needed peace and quiet to recover, they told him. So he took their suggestion, moved to Banff, and stayed there for the rest of his life. He never said much about the Tilikum. Certainly he didn't write about it until his daughter pestered him into revising his journals many years later. Maybe he wanted to forget it; maybe he just had other things to do.

In 1904, he married Georgia Elizabeth McDougall, his "second princess," the daughter of David McDougall. You don't hear so much about that particular branch of the McDougall family, but his brother, Rev. John McDougall, and father, Rev. George McDougall, devoted their lives to establishing the Methodist church in western Canada. Indeed, Georgia was the first white child born in the area that eventually bore the name Alberta. When she was born to David and Annie McDougall on her grandfather's mission east of Edmonton in 1870, the area was called the Northwest Territories and the mission was called the Victoria Mission. Eventually the name of the area was changed to Alberta, and the mission was renamed Pakan in honour of an Indian leader who lived nearby. When the mission closed, however, there was nothing left that needed a name, though the name Pakan remains on her grave and in the history books.

Luxton became one of Banff's biggest boosters. He bought the newspaper, he helped organize Banff Indian Days, and he built the King

Edward Hotel. In between times and at all times, he collected Indian artifacts, stuffed animals and birds, memorabilia of the early days of Banff. Eventually his collection became the Luxton Museum.

Because of his interest in the Indians and their culture, both Norman and Georgia were given honorary titles by the Indians in the Banff area, and that explains a line of Cree on the bottom of their gravemarker. When translated, it means: **"Remove not the ancient land mark which thy fathers have set."**

~

The message on Stephan Stephansson's grave in Markerville echoes the words of the Cree message on the Luxton grave except that it's written in English and Icelandic, which goes to show, once again, that we may come from different places and speak different languages, but our words are remarkably similar! This is the English translation of the Icelandic words:

> *Though you have trodden in travel*
> *All the wide tracts of the earth*
> *Bear yet the dreams of your bosom*
> *Back to the land of your birth.*

The land of Stephansson's birth was Iceland. When he moved to Canada and homesteaded near Markerville, he worked on the family farm during the day, but at night he put on his other cap and wrote poetry. Because he wrote in his native language and published in his native country, Canadians knew very little about the poet in their midst. Even after he was honoured in his homeland with awards and a triumphal tour, Stephansson continued to be more or less invisible in Canada.

That all changed in the 1980s when the Alberta government decided to turn the Stephansson house and farmyard into a historic site, complete with sign boards and paved paths and young ladies in period costume who earnestly retell the life and times of Alberta's famous poet. It's done well, and it's high time the story was told, but a story of another sort is told in the family graveyard about a mile west of the house. As might be expected, it is dominated by a large stone cairn in memory of the now famous poet. However, near the father's grave is a much smaller one in memory of Gestur Stephansson, one of eight children born to Stephan and his wife, Helga.

In the summer of 1909, sixteen-year-old Gestur and his two broth-ers got caught in a swift summer storm and raced for the safety of home. Gestur reached the gate first, but just as he touched the barbed wire to open the gate, lightning struck. The full force of its electricity travelled down the wire, and Gestur was killed instantly.

Stephan Stephansson delivered the eulogy at his son's funeral:

To us his parents, he was precious, to his brothers and sisters, a good brother. I never knew him intentionally to hurt anyone. Had he lived longer, he would have become more of a man, but never a better one. For him, I would have no misgivings...He has enriched our remembrances, and although it is so very painful to lose him, the void in my life would have been far more grievous if he had never been mine and if I had never known the enjoyment of his company.

Gestur was buried on the farm, on a slight rise surrounded by poplar trees. Stephansson referred to the spot in a poem years later as a "greening hill amid the trees," and when he died in 1927, he too was laid to rest on the greening hill. It is not part of the tourist trappings further down the road.

~

There are two graves in Indian Battle Park in Lethbridge, however, that are part of a tourist attraction. At first, I wondered about keeping them there. Surely, I thought as I drove the twists and turns of that large park area, monuments to death in the midst of picnic tables and teeter totters are a bit of a downer. And maybe a recreational area isn't exactly the place to foster the sort of respect that graves ought to get, and so on. I was as confused about the whole idea as I was about the exact location of the graves. But when I found them, I also found two young boys. They were ten or so, apparently not affected by the fact that it was as hot a day as you'd ever want to experience in southern Alberta. Even the grass-hoppers had taken the afternoon off and crawled under the nearby cottonwood trees for some shelter from the sun. But the boys stayed out in the open area around the graves. There they read the tourist informa-tion next to the graves, then they teetered on the chains strung around the graves, then kicked around a bit of the shale on the nearby paths.

When they came back to their dad, who sat reading a book in the

42

shade, they seemed puzzled, "Why did that guy have to die?" they asked. "He was only seventeen years old."

Then and there I decided that the city fathers and mothers had done exactly the right thing in leaving the graves where they were. How we die is part of our story; why hide it behind thick caragana hedges and fuzzy liberal fears? Better that these boys — who had the fortitude to ignore the heat in order to process some of the unhappier parts of our past — better they should ask the questions and learn the answers.

The seventeen-year-old buried in the heart of Indian Battle Park is Henry Stafford, who died before western Canada had barely begun, at least as settled history is measured. His father, William Stafford, was the first mines superintendent of the North Western Coal and Navigation Company, the company that was bound and determined to get rich mining the coal seams in the hills around what is now called Lethbridge but what was then called Coalbanks. Two of the investors in the company were Sir Alexander Galt, one of the Fathers of Confederation and a member of the federal government, and William Lethbridge, a wealthy British investor who never even set foot in the town that was named for him.

It was all very exciting, establishing this brand new industry in a brand new town. But there's a down side to every new settlement, and in this case, it was typhoid fever, the disease that claimed young Henry Stafford.

There were no burial grounds in Coalbanks in 1883, so Henry's dad selected a spot down on the river bank near several groves of cottonwood trees. Maybe that's why he selected the river bank. The site of Lethbridge on the benchlands above didn't get trees until later, when people planted them and stood guard over their growth. A month after Henry's death, a young workman named Britton Stephens also succumbed to typhoid and joined young Henry under the cottonwoods.

In the next few years, a registered graveyard was established nearer the town site, but somehow Henry and Britton never got moved. They stayed, summer and winter, down on the river bank, more or less forgotten. But they're in the thick of things now, a tourist attraction and a reason for little boys to ask good questions about our history.

～

I can think of a lot of good questions to ask about Alberta's Famous Five, the women who changed the Canadian constitution without so much as a referendum or murmur in the press, but the main one is why? Why aren't their accomplishments mentioned on their gravemarkers? Why don't their graves say in big bold letters — Canadian Heroes?

Four of the five Alberta women who went to bat for Canadian women as a whole, fighting for our right to be known as "persons" under the law, are silent on their gravemarkers about that particular achievement. The fifth is not. Emily Murphy is marked by more words than anybody else in the Edmonton Mausoleum, and I guess that will have to tell the story for all of them.

> *Emily Ferguson Murphy (Janey Canuck)*
> *Beloved wife of Rev. Arthur Murphy. MA*
> *Daughter of Isaac and Emily Ferguson*
> *Born at Cookstown, Ont., March 14, 1868*
> *Died at Edmonton, AB. October 26, 1933*
> *Decorated by His Majesty King George V,*
> *A Lady Of Grace of the Order of*
> *St. John of Jerusalem in 1914.*
> *First woman in the British Empire to be*
> *Appointed a Police magistrate*
> *Being also judge of the juvenile court for province of Alberta*
> *Originator and Leader of movement admitting women*
> *To the Senate of Canada*
> *Author, jurist, crusader in social reforms, great citizen.*
> *"As when a standard bearer fainteth." Isaiah X, 18*

That pretty well sums it up. Emily Murphy was one busy, strong, determined, ambitious woman who tackled injustice whenever and wherever she could — serving as magistrate and judge in women's courts, advocating improved laws for woman and often actually rewriting those laws for the legislators, serving on every kind of committee and task force that tackled social issues. In turn, she expected a little appreciation. She really had her heart set on being appointed the first woman to sit in Canada's Senate, but time and time again, her nomination was turned down because "she was not a person according to the BNA Act."

She finally found a way to challenge that tired old argument, and she went for it, but she had to have a total of five "persons" acting as a unit to sign the Supreme Court petition. The other "persons" that she selected were Nellie McClung, Irene Parlby, Louise McKinney, and Henrietta Muir Edwards. They met at Emily Murphy's house in Edmonton one summer afternoon in 1927 and enthusiastically sent the petition on its way. Nellie McClung spoke for them all when she said, "God bless our Cause and confound the enemy."

It took two years and a final appeal to the Privy Council of England, but on October 18, 1929, they finally heard that Canadian women were, in fact, "persons" under the law and as such could be senators. And that was the end of that hurtful episode in Canadian history — except that Emily Murphy never did get called to the Canadian Senate. In 1933, four short years later, she died at the age of sixty-five. I say it was heartbreak, but then I'm prejudiced.

Nellie McClung, the favourite of everyone, author of numerous books, the one feminist who could sweeten her message with a flashing wit and genuine warmth, is buried in Victoria, B.C., in the Royal Oak Burial Park. Her epitaph is a clipped "**Loved and Remembered**," both of which are true, of course, but so much more could be said.

Louise McKinney, with her Women's Christian Temperance Union connections and her record as the first woman ever to sit in a provincial legislature, shares a gravemarker with her husband in the Claresholm Cemetery. His side says "**Father**;" hers reads "**Mother**."

Irene Parlby, who was an Alberta MLA and first female cabinet minister in the British Empire, is buried in the Alix Cemetery. Her gravestone acknowledges an LL.B. from the University of Alberta, but that's all.

Henrietta Muir Edwards is not buried in Fort Macleod, where she spent the last years of her life, but with her son and husband in the Mount Pleasant Cemetery in Edmonton. The inscription on her gravemarker hints that she might have been interested in laws: "**Let her works praise her/ Her delight was in the law of the Lord.**" But of the group, only Emily Murphy tells some of the story.

∾

Sometimes it isn't the words but the images on a gravestone that tell the story, or at least hint that there's a story to be told. Certainly the metal cutout of a steam engine chugging and smoking its way across Ashley Butterwick's concrete grave cover piqued my imagination. Add to that the words "**An Artist Rests**," and it practically demanded an explanation. Was it the grave of a railroad man who painted pretty pictures in his spare time? Was it the other way around, an artist who liked painting trains? Or was it just one of the few fanciful images to be found in Alberta's graveyards? The truth turned out to be more interesting than any of my fictions.

The artist in question was Ashley Butterwick, who came from England in 1908 with his parents and settled in the Lethbridge area, where his dad managed to lose a fair-sized fortune in just two years. "This," said Butterwick in a story he wrote years later, "caused my mother to dislike this country violently." Small wonder.

Butterwick learned very early to scramble for a living, a skill that he needed more than ever after his wife died, leaving him with four youngsters. He had to stay close to home to look after them, so he applied his scrambling techniques — a little sign painting here, some road work there, janitor work everywhere. How he had time for anything else is the real question, but he did. He built model steam engines just for the fun of it, and he was very good at it. Two of his finished ones he put into a miniature train and boat ride for the kids in Nemiscan where he was living, and one he put into the first train in Bowness Park east of Calgary. Several others were displayed at exhibitions across Canada, and one went all the way to London, England, for an international model contest in 1938.

The engine that he sent to the competition was quite a complicated affair: a seventy-five-pound pound steam engine capable of burning either coal or alcohol, its back wheels a jigsaw puzzle of seventy-two separate pieces, and the whole thing painted and trimmed with great care. Unfortunately, it didn't arrive in time for the 1938 competition, so the organizers agreed to keep it for the next year. That was nice of them, because Butterwick's engine won second prize in its category that year. Then it was crated up, put on a boat and sent home to Canada.

It never arrived, but that wasn't too surprising. By that time, we were in the midst of World War II, and Butterwick concluded that the boat had been lost at sea. So much for the little engine that could.

Twenty years later, he received a letter from a shipping company in

London telling him they had a package addressed to him. They were just getting around to some of their back mail now that the war was over. Did he still want it? Of course he did. The long lost engine finally found its way home, apparently none the worse for wear and war: it worked just fine.

When Butterwick died in 1974, it was son Bill who decided his father ought to have an engine on his gravemarker. He made a cutout of solid steel and mounted it on the concrete cover, then added the rings of smoke by cutting pieces from three different sized pipes. "Dad was a character," he said. "I thought his grave should have some character too."

The little engine that could went to the museum at Etzikom.

~

The grave of artist Lars Jonson Haukaness is one of the few that actually admits artistic connections. Artists generally prefer anonymity, silence, humility to the end, and Haukaness would likely have gone the same route except that he died before his time and others made decisions for him. As a result, in the old graveyard at Banff, there's an original bronze relief, a mountain scene, mounted on a slab of mountain rock at the head of Haukaness's grave. Another plaque, located at the foot of the grave, reads:

Lars Jonson Haukaness, 1862-1929,
Born in Granvin, Hardanger, Norway.
First Professional Art Instructor
Provincial Institute of Technology and Art, Calgary
Died on a Painting Excursion in the Ptarmigan Valley
This plaque modelled by Euphemia McNaught in 1931
Was dedicated on September 7, 1985.

Not surprisingly, many of the bronze plaques in the Banff graveyard feature mountains and horses, and so it is with Lars Haukaness' grave, but in this case the mountain scene is not from the Rockies around Banff. It was modelled by artist Euphemia McNaught and was part of her memories about growing up in the countryside near the Rockies in northern Alberta. She lives there still, on a farm near Beaverlodge that her father homesteaded in 1912 after he came to the country via the terrible Edson

47

Trail. She still talks about the oxen that made that trip, Josh and Johnny, as if they were right out there in the corrals behind the house, and she has painted them from memory numerous times.

She's in her eighties now, lives with her sister in a house that couldn't hold one more thing if they tried — and they will — and over the chesterfield in the sunroom is the original plaster cast of the horses and rider, and mountains in the background, that was used for Haukaness. Out in the porch is a bronze rendition of the same.

Lars Jonson Haukaness had a significant impact on the art scene in Alberta, but he's no household word. He came to Calgary in 1926 as an instructor for the Provincial Institute of Technology and Art, known for years as the "Tech." He was sixty-four years old by then and had worked as an artist in his native Norway and then all over the United States and Canada without much success or recognition. He was kind of a lonesome soul, always alone, often on the move. For the three years that he taught at the Tech, he talked up the need for an art school that would be separate from the technical school, one that would have its own budget and curriculum. His wasn't the only voice on this issue, but it was an insistent one. The idea of a provincial art school began to take root.

One of the people he interviewed for a teaching position at that time was a recent graduate of the Ontario College of Art, Euphemia McNaught. She had never applied for a job before and was terribly nervous about her interview with Haukaness. What would she say? She was just a kid from the Peace River country who seemed to have some talent in her fingers. Her aunt in Calgary advised her to calm down and just tell him what she knew.

The advice worked, and the interview went very well. But Miss McNaught remembered that Haukaness seemed to be the saddest man she had ever met. "Imagine," she said, "to be so lonely that you show a stranger some of your drawings and souvenirs of the old country." He also told her about the pack trip that he was planning to take into the Rocky Mountains to gather sketches for future paintings. She, in turn, told him about some of her pack trips in the Monkman Pass further north in the Rockies near her home in Beaverlodge. They parted the best of friends, and Miss McNaught thought she had the job. That was the spring of 1929.

In the summer of 1929, Haukaness headed for the mountains on his long-awaited sketching trip. As usual, he was alone, accompanied only by his dog and a pack horse. A Calgarian who met him on his way west said, "He was full of enthusiasm...he reminded me of Don Quixote making preparations for a journey of adventure." Some days later, Haukaness's dog led searchers to his master's body. He had died of an apparent heart attack while working in his favourite location, the Ptarmigan Valley near Lake Louise. The burial took place in the Banff Cemetery a few days later.

That might have been the end of the story had the Sons of Norway not decided some years later that their countryman should be marked with a certain amount of ceremony. After all, he had been an artist of some note. Attention should be paid. They contacted Euphemia McNaught and asked her if she had anything they could use to mark Haukaness's grave.

That's how her design became the bronze relief at the head of the grave. At the unveiling of the bronze on September 7, 1985, various officials spoke, including one from the now independent and widely respected Alberta College of Art in Calgary. "You see, he was right," Euphemia McNaught said later. "He knew that art has to have its own place."

~

A horse is featured on another famous Alberta gravemarker, and although there's no guarantee that the horse pictured on the gravemarker is the infamous Cyclone, it should be. Cyclone was the bucking horse that Tom Three Persons rode in the very first Calgary Stampede. By hanging on for what seemed like an eternity, Tom Three Persons ensured himself a place in cowboy history and the right to say on his gravemarker: **"World's Champion Bronco Buster, September 1912, Calgary, Alberta."**

It's such a good story, all the more because nobody could have predicted it. Tom Three Persons was just a local cowboy from the Blood reserve in southern Alberta. How could he compete with the professionals who had been lured up from the States to take part in the very first Stampede? He wasn't in shape; he'd just gotten out of jail in Fort Macleod where he had been "resting" after too much celebrating. Who could nurse a hangover and ride a bucking bronco too?

The first day of the first Stampede, September 12, 1912, Tom Three Persons drew the horse called Carrie Nation. If the original Carrie Nation had had anything to do with it, Tom Three Persons would not have been able to complete his ride. Fierce temperance fighter that she was, Carrie

Nation would have had something to say about men who drink. But in a delicious bit of irony, Tom Three Persons got a good ride. The next time he competed, he drew "Speckled Face." Again he had a good ride and scored well.

By Saturday, most of the finalists in the bucking horse class were the more experienced American cowboys. It was beginning to look like an American rout. Only five Albertans had stuck it out, and when Tom Three Persons drew the dreaded Cyclone, everybody figured he was out as well. Nobody could outlast Cyclone. Tom was pretty much of the same opinion. As he watched the men move his wild horse into the chutes, he said aloud that he didn't think he could ever stay on. But another cowboy told him not to be fooled by Cyclone's antics. "When he stands up on his hind legs and teeters backwards, as if he's going to fall backwards, don't be fooled," the other cowboy told him. "It's just part of his act." So Tom hung on tight the whole time, never once letting up. And it worked. He rode Cyclone to the finish.

The crowd went crazy. Not only had Cyclone been bested, but he had been bested by one of their own. Tom Three Persons was the Bucking Horse Champion of the World. He got a medal, he got $1000, he got a handmade saddle and a championship belt buckle.

He also got to go back to Fort Macleod and finish off his jail sentence.

In the next few years, he continued to compete in rodeos in Canada and the United States, but he never got that big one again, the big ride that would make a whole country sit up and take notice. He eventually settled down on his land near Cardston and raised purebred Herefords and race horses.

In 1949, at sixty-three years of age, Tom Three Persons died and was buried in the cemetery behind St. Mary's Catholic Church on the Blood Reserve. With him went his medals and a great source of pride for the community. The largest funeral procession ever seen at St. Mary's Church wound its way home after the service.

~

Twelve Foot Davis had an interesting life and deserves a place in this book because of that fact alone, but his grave is now more famous than he is. It's not what Davis intended when he asked his old buddy Peace

River Jim Cornwall to bury him on top of the Peace River hills "when the time comes," but that's what has happened.

It's too bad. It's about the most beautiful grave site in all of Alberta, a "greening hill," to quote Stephan Stephansson, that overlooks the Peace and Smoky Rivers where they join to form one mighty river. The river wanders along in its gentle valley right in front of Twelve Foot Davis, a 180 degree sweep from south to north. In the winter, the river and its valley are white on white with the occasional spruce tree providing contrast. In the summer, it's green on green with hardly anything to provide contrast except, of course, the town of Peace River which, if you lean forward far enough, you can also see from Twelve Foot Davis's location. He picked well, did Davis.

Twelve Foot Davis doesn't seem to have had a regular name. His initials were F.H., but he's never referred to in any of the literature as anything but "Twelve Foot." Even on the original map showing placer claims on Williams Lake during the Cariboo gold rush, he is listed as 12 Ft. Davis, so he must have earned his gold and his nickname by then. Both came about because he was smart enough to notice that two mining claims took up a total of 212 feet, when they were allowed to take up only 100 feet each, a total of 200 feet. Thus, there had to be a 12 foot space between the two claims. Davis filed on that space and made himself a tidy $12,000. In the 1860s, that was a lot of money.

A few years later, Davis hit the road again and ended up in the Peace River country. He liked what he saw, so he stayed for the rest of his life and became a "free" trader, bringing in goods from British Columbia or Edmonton and trading them for furs or money. Later he would sell the furs to established traders such as the Hudson's Bay Company and get himself some more money to do some more trading, and so on. It was a great way to remain independent and see the country, staying now and then at the various trading posts that he built up and down the river. The term "trading post" is actually a bit grand for the establishments of Twelve Foot Davis. They were small shacks used to store trading goods, and they were never locked. If travellers needed something, they simply helped themselves, and the accounts were squared up later. It's no wonder that he built a reputation as an honest and generous man.

For the last part of his life, he lived at the Anglican Mission at what was then called Lesser Slave Lake but is now known as Grouard. One of the Anglican sisters, perhaps hoping to ease his mind about the hereafter, asked him if he was frightened of dying. Not at all, he said, "I never killed nobody, I never stole from nobody and I always kept open-house for all travellers all my life. No, miss, I ain't afraid to die."

He was originally buried at the Anglican mission, but Jim Cornwall, remembering his promise to his friend, had him brought back to Peace River and buried on the hill with the best view in the world. He saw to it that a fairly grand gravemarker was erected with a plaque on it that said, **"Pathfinder, Pioneer, Miner and Trader. He was every man's friend and never locked his cabin door."** The first gravemarker from Grouard stands in front of the Peace River Museum now, with the wrong dates on it. Davis died in 1900, not 1893 as it says on the first marker.

And that should have been the end of the story — friend keeps a promise and buries friend. But the gravemarker on the hill became a tourist attraction and a handy place for late night drinking parties. Pretty soon there wasn't much left of Jim Cornwall's tribute to his friend. Vandals broke what they could and spray painted the rest. Eventually the town had to replace the replacement, and what is up on the hill now is a concrete bunker with some of the original stones and an interpretive sign that includes the original inscription. What a shame that a man who never locked his doors in his lifetime has had to be turned into a concrete fortress in his death.

Still, the spectacular view remains, and a river runs through it.

∿

THE LAST WORD: It's short but it's sweet, and it tells a good story. It's the epitaph on the gravemarker of Hulbert (Hullie) Henry Orser, 1897-1981, in the Earlville Rutherford Cemetery near Ponoka.

He feared God, did nothing mean
Shot straight and stayed clean.

∿

Stories That Don't Make it Into the Graveyard

Gone Higher

...words that were supposed to go on the gravemarker
of mountaineer Norman Bethune Sanson in the
Banff Cemetery but somehow never got there.
It figures.

The more I saw of our graveyards, the more frustrated I became with western humility and modesty. "For heaven's sake," I would say, as I stood in front of the grave of someone important to our history, 'Speak up. Say something.' But no, some of our best stories are untold, our best heroes and heroines unsung. What a loss.

Take, for example, Norman Bethune Sanson. He climbed Sulphur Mountain in Banff every week, winter and summer, to check on the observatory there. He made his last climb when he was a spry eighty-three years old, and a few years later, the Geographic Board of Canada named the peak on which the observatory stood "Sanson Peak." He was an incredibly interesting character, but could we guess that from looking at his gravemarker in the Banff Cemetery? Not a chance. How much better it would be if the gravemarker did indeed say "Gone Higher." At least there would be a hint that we should look for more information about Sanson.

Then there's Chief Crowfoot. When I visited his final resting place in the Cluny Cemetery, I kept wondering why there wasn't more. After all, Crowfoot is just about the most famous, the most respected of all Indian leaders in western Canada. I thought his grave site would be marked with some sort of grandeur. But it's just a lonely little grave enclosed by an iron grille fence out on the southern tip of the Cluny graveyard. The small metal marker says on the one side:

Chief Crowfoot
Died April 26, 1890
Aged 69 yrs.

On the other side is written: "**Father of Our People**."

There are plans to upgrade the area with more signs, an interpretive centre, a picnic and campsite on the valley below, but for the time being, it's surprisingly stark.

When Crowfoot was first buried, the Catholic priest and the Indian agent wanted the casket to be buried in the Christian tradition, completely covered with earth, but his Blackfoot people wanted it to remain above ground so that his spirit would be free to enter the spirit world. It's a good thing that Crowfoot was used to compromise during his lifetime, because a compromise was worked out on the occasion of his death as well. His casket was put half in, half out of the ground, and a spirit house was built over it. Some years later, the graveyard was cleaned up and organized, and Crowfoot was reburied, this time completely underground.

The most splendid thing about Crowfoot's last resting place is the location, and perhaps that is as it should be. The prairie stretches as far as the eye can see on three sides, beige velvet hills with only the grain elevators of Cluny, like little toy buildings in the distance, breaking up the horizon. On the fourth side, looking south and down, is Blackfoot Crossing, the wide valley of the Bow where the Indians of southern Alberta came together so many years ago to sign Treaty #7.

By the time the treaty was signed, Crowfoot was regarded as the most important leader in southern Alberta, even though technically he had no more rank than many other chiefs in the area. But Crowfoot had the words. He was the Churchill of his time and race. At the Treaty #7 signing he said to the assembled government and church officials:

Great Father! Take pity on me with regard to my country, with regard to the mountains, the hills and the valleys; with regard to the prairies, the forests and the waters; with regard to all the animals that inhabit them, and do not take them from myself and my children for ever.

And when he and several other Blackfoot chiefs were taken by Lieutenant Governor Edgar Dewdney on a train trip to Winnipeg, Crowfoot looked long and hard at all the people, all the streets and buildings creeping outward over the prairies, and he told his people, "It is useless to rise against the white. They are as plentiful as the flies in summertime."

Even on his deathbed, he made a most beautiful speech. Of course he did — he had been making beautiful speeches all his life. Unfortunately there is no solid proof that he actually said what he has been credited with saying. Dr. Henry George, who attended Crowfoot in his last hours, did not mention the famous speech in his report; nor did the *Calgary Herald* in its extensive coverage of the death. Still, the words are lovely, and history can afford to be generous. This is what Crowfoot is supposed to have said just before he died in April, 1890:

> A little while and I will be gone from among you, whither I cannot tell. From nowhere we come, into nowhere we go. What is life? It is a flash of firefly in the night. It is a breath of a buffalo in the wintertime. It is as the little shadow that runs across the grass and loses itself in the sunset.

A few days later, Father Leon Doucet conducted a full Catholic burial service for Chief Crowfoot, claiming that he had been baptized in the Catholic faith and would have wanted it that way. J.W. Tims, an Anglican minister who also served among the Indians of southern Alberta, wasn't quite so sure about that. "He died as he had lived in the faith of his father," Tims said, pointing out that Crowfoot's favourite horse had been shot upon his death so that Crowfoot might ride it in the spirit world. That didn't sound like regulation Christian practice to Tims. But what did it matter? The argument between the two Christian churches was just so many words, like flies in summertime. The truth needed no words — the mighty Crowfoot was dead.

∽

Now we all know that Sam McGee was from Tennessee where the cotton blooms and blows, right? And we all know how he was cremated on the marge of Lake Lebarge, right?

Wrong. The real Sam McGee never got anywhere near Tennessee, although he certainly did cover a lot of miles in his lifetime. And the land of gold didn't hold him like a spell, even though he couldn't resist one last prospecting trip years after he'd left the area for good. And for sure, he wasn't cremated. Truth is, the real Sam McGee wasn't at all like the one in the poem. The only thing they shared was the same name.

William Samuel McGee was born in Ontario in 1867, the year that Canada became a confederation. He was known as William until he arrived in Whitehorse in 1898. Every other man there seemed to have a shortened no-nonsense name — Jack or Big Mike or Barb Wire Bill — so William became Sam. He did his banking at the Canadian Bank of Commerce, where one of the tellers was a young man named Robert Service who happened to write poetry in his spare time. One day Robert Service was trying to come up with a name for a character in one of his poems, a name that would rhyme with Tennessee, when who should appear at his wicket but Sam McGee. Perfect. He checked with Sam, and Sam said sure, use my name, and the rest is history.

Robert Service was never terribly proud of "The Cremation of Sam McGee" and "The Shooting of Dan McGrew," but they had such swing and down-to-earth language that everyone else loved them. Although he wrote many more books of poetry and prose, nothing else caught on like those two originals. He got rich on them and lived his last years in comparative splendour in France.

Not so for the real Sam McGee. He left the Yukon in 1909 and moved around for the next thirty years, farming here, growing fruit there, building roads everywhere. He was best at road construction and could generally find work of that kind, but he never forgot the North either. He vowed that someday, he would make his big strike. His chance came in 1938, when he was living in Great Falls, Montana. A friend with a small plane delivered Sam and a companion to the Liard River area north of Whitehorse. They planned to spend the summer exploring and come out in the fall with bags full of gold — rich beyond belief. It didn't quite work that way. All that Sam brought out with him was a bag of his own ashes. When he visited Whitehorse at the end of the prospecting trip, he discovered that his old cabin there had been spruced up as a tourist attraction, and one of the items being offered for sale in the gift shop was "Genuine Sam McGee ashes." Not only had he died, according to the tourist bureau of Whitehorse, but he had been such a massive man that his ashes would apparently supply the tourist demand for some time. Who could resist? He bought some. Another sign urged visitors to have a cup of tea with the ghost of Sam McGee.

Come to think of it, it's like the Robert Service poem. In the poem, his fictional counterpart was written off prematurely — he was expected to be dead in the heart of the furnace roar. But he wasn't. "Please close that door," he said. "Since I left Plumtree, down in Tennessee, it's the first time I've been warm."

Meanwhile, the real Sam McGee and his wife Ruth moved in with their married daughter, Mrs. Emil Gramms of Beiseker. Sam would have opened a motel in British Columbia in the fall after his trip to the North — that was his next plan — but he got kicked by a bull and didn't seem to get his strength back. Then his heart started acting up, and he couldn't get around very well. And then he died, for real.

His grave is in the Seventh Day Adventist Church Cemetery about ten miles east and south of Beiseker. The marker doesn't tell us anything about its interesting namesake. You'd never even know it was Sam. It says William.

~

Alberta artists are also silent in the graveyard, so silent you'd hardly know we had any. You can find reference to soldiers, farmers, storekeepers, cowboys, and politicians, but about artists, whether in music, visual arts, writing, or theatre, there's hardly a word.

Some moved away, of course, like the artist William Kurelek who grew up in Ukrainian country around Willingdon but is buried in Toronto. Others have chosen cremation. In fact, a lot of people in the arts have selected cremation over the years, to be followed by the scattering of ashes over some favourite and original spot like a mountain top or a fishing hole or a secret garden. And while it must be granted that everyone has the right to choose — if nothing else in life — their resting place after death, it does leave the graveyards somewhat bereft of artistic history, as if Alberta had never sheltered artists in its midst.

Take Odette De Foras, for example. The daughter of French immigrants who settled on a ranch outside of High River in 1907, Odette wanted to be an opera singer. But how? Training wasn't available in western Canada; anywhere else would have cost too much money. Odette solved the problem herself by winning a scholarship to the Royal Academy of Music in London, England, where she studied for four years.

From 1922 to 1932, she performed at Covent Garden, once receiving a standing ovation at a command performance for King George and Queen Mary. Tickets for that performance sold for as much as 100 pounds each, but whenever Miss De Foras returned to High River, she would sing for much less at local concerts and benefits. Always in her repertoire she would include Hermann Lohr's "Little Grey Home in the West" for her mother, she explained, who loved the sentimental old song.

In the 1930s, Miss De Foras came back to High River to recuperate from an illness, and before she could get back to Europe, war was declared. Travel was impossible. More and more, she and her sister took over management of the family farm. In the fall of 1958, as she was planning and training for a comeback, fire broke out in their ranch house. She raced for help, but it was no use. A chinook wind was blowing, and the house burned before anyone could even find a pail, let alone water. "At first my piano was standing tall and erect. Then suddenly it was no more," she remembered years later. "There was only one thing to do. I put back my head and I sang." The song that she sang was, of course, "Little Grey Home in the West."

Odette de Foras never did make the comeback she had hoped for. She gave a concert at the Jubilee Auditorium in Calgary the next year, but she didn't go back to Europe. She lived quietly in High River until her death in 1976. Her grave there is absolutely mute. As a singer, she once told a newspaper reporter, you must "Keep your mind on the note you're going to sing and go right to it." That should have been on her gravemarker.

~

Nicholas De Grandmaison is also buried without a word of explanation. He is in the Peigan graveyard at Brocket, west of Pincher Creek. The grey granite cross mounted on a matching base looks as if it might signal a person of substance, but all it says is "Nicholas De Grandmaison, Chief Little Plume, February 24, 1897- March 23, 1978." Not a word about his art and the fact that collectors lined up and paid the world for one of his Indian portraits.

De Grandmaison came to Canada from Russia in 1923, and after discovering that farm work was not meant for him, he discovered that Indians were. He had worked as a graphic artist in his native country and liked the "pure" Indian faces he found in western Canada. He decided to put the two together, especially after he discovered that there was a market for the combination. He could do landscapes until he was blue in the face and they would remain unsold, but do one Indian portrait and he would make a sale. His pastel and oil paintings eventually became so popular that he couldn't keep up with the demand.

He was not particularly interested in his Indian subjects as people, only as faces, but the Indians liked him anyway. Even if he didn't understand that they weren't always proud, independent and noble — the way he saw them through his rose-coloured glasses — they preferred his interpretation. In 1959, De Grandmaison was named an honorary chief of the Peigan band and given the name Chief Little Plume, the name that went with him to the grave.

~

Roland Gissing's grave in Queen's Park Cemetery in Calgary at least hints at his talent. It's a substantial slab of stone with a bronze plaque mounted on the front of it, a combination that immediately attracts attention because it breaks the monotony of the look-alike black granite markers all around it. The plaque is simply designed and includes a stylized tree on one side, his name signed as it was on all his famous western landscapes, and the dates, 1895-1967.

When Gissing came to Canada from England in 1913, he came because he thought it would be fun to be a cowboy, to ride horse all day, sing cowboy songs around the campfire at night, chew tobacco. He was eighteen years old, and the cowboy's life sounded pretty good to him. With his very first paycheque, earned on a farm near Calgary, he bought woolly chaps and a slicker from Riley and McCormick. He may not have been a cowboy yet, but he knew what to wear. For the next ten years, he wandered around the West. Sometimes he got work as a cowboy; sometimes not. Sometimes he lived in a house; sometimes not. He ended up back in the Calgary area, and this time he got himself a homestead in the Ghost River area and settled down to farm. Also to paint.

His first one-man show was held in Calgary in 1929, but he didn't go into the business of painting until five years later — and "business" is the right word. He had no intention of starving in a garret for "the sake of his art." He analyzed his market, realized what would sell, then produced it. As luck would have it, what would sell was also what was in front of his nose: mountains, lakes, rivers, trees, fields, especially harvest fields with stooks of grain in them.

Gissing learned to paint bigger canvases for Calgary markets be-cause Calgarians were bigger spenders. His smaller canvases went to Edmonton and other more modest markets. If a canvas didn't sell the first time around, he would bring it home and add colour. "Buyers can't resist colour," he explained. "I'm a businessman. I give the people what they want, it's as simple as that."

Even though he called himself a businessman and not an artist, he was like other artists in that he was never satisfied with his work. He would like a bit of one painting and a part of another but never the whole. If he really didn't like it, he'd use it for something else. A neighbour once spied a Gissing original covering a window of the chicken coop in the back yard. There may be one like it somewhere in Buckingham Palace. One of Gissing's paintings was presented to the then Princess Elizabeth and the Duke of Edinburgh on a royal visit. Gissing was invited to the party, but he declined.

He died in 1967. Art critics never had much praise for Gissing — he was far too commercial for their tastes — but on the occasion of his death, one did admit, "If ever a man sold Alberta, it was Gissing."

~

I know that premiers and lieutenant-governors are only the tip of the iceberg when it comes to the political history of a province, but I was curious nonetheless to see what was written on the tombstones of our most prominent politicians. If our artists are quiet on their gravemarkers, what about our politicians? Would their tombstones tell us anything about themselves or the province? Would service as a premier or lieutenant-governor be a source of pride and therefore mentioned on the gravemarker? And if not, why not? After a lot of tramping around the graveyards and numerous letters, I can report that Alberta politicians do not make much of their public service.

A.C. Rutherford, the province's first premier, is buried in the Mount Pleasant graveyard in southern Edmonton and has the sort of substan-tial tombstone one expects of a political leader. Located on top of a hill, the gravestone has "**Premier of Alberta 1905-1910**" clearly indicated below his name and dates. Lest we ever forget that public figures have as many heartaches as the rest of us, there is also in the shadow of the big Rutherford marker a small one that says simply, "**Our Babe.**"

Also buried in Edmonton, in the Evergreen Memorial Gardens east of the city, but completely tight-lipped about his political past is John Brownlee, who as leader of the United Farmers of Alberta served as premier for nearly nine years, 1925-34. Brownlee's reticence is somewhat understandable in that he left politics under a cloud of scandal. In 1933, he was accused of the seduction of a young government clerk named Vivian MacMillan, and in spite of protests from all who knew him, including his wife, that he could not possibly have done such a thing, he was found guilty and forced to pay damages both to the girl and her father.

The trial was rivetting for a whole lot of reasons, not the least of which was that it dealt with sex, a subject not generally mentioned in polite society in those days. Then, too, it was a scandal among people in high places. The newspapers couldn't keep up with the demand for details. They finally just printed the entire court transcript and let everybody read everything. In the end, it was never clear just who was telling the truth about what, and that added to the public interest. Brownlee may have been innocent, but why did he take Miss MacMillan on all those late night drives? Vivian MacMillan, for her part, may have been guilty of deception, but why didn't that fact leak out in later years? It remains one of our best mysteries. Of course, his grave doesn't breathe a word of it.

When Brownlee finally had to leave politics, his fellow legislator R.G. Reid finished out the term, 1934-35. Then the Social Credit party came out of nowhere and surprised everyone. Reid may have served the shortest term of any Alberta premier, but he lived the longest. He died in 1980 at the age of 101 and is buried in the Edmonton Cemetery under a flush marker so plain as to be invisible.

Arthur Lewis Sifton, who served as premier from 1910 to 1917, and his successor Charles Stewart, 1917-21, are both buried in the Beechwood Cemetery in Ottawa. Neither of their gravemarkers mentions Alberta. Herbert Greenfield, premier from 1921 to 1925, is buried in Calgary's Union Cemetery. Had he been buried in the Edmonton graveyard with his first wife, where a large Greenfield granite marker awaited him, he might have had a few words written about him. As it is, he is marked by the plainest, most no-nonsense bronze flush marker you can find. His second wife has a similarly plain marker beside him. Another silent grave that you have to look long and hard for belongs to Harry Strom, premier from 1968 to 1971, who is buried in the Medicine Hat Chapel Lawn Cemetery.

And William Aberhart, who made such a difference to the province of Alberta, isn't even buried here. The Social Credit leader who took the province by storm in 1935 is buried in Burnaby, British Columbia, partly because his family was mad at Alberta and the way Albertans had treated him. His flush gravemarker is about as anonymous as a gravemarker could be, but it does include the terse information, "**Premier of Alberta 1935-1943.**" By my reckoning, that means that two of Alberta's premiers admitted to their political life, and one did so reluctantly.

As for lieutenant-governors, they don't exactly boast about their regal responsibilities either. The first one, G.H.V. Bulyea, who served from 1905 to 1915, is buried in Qu'Appelle, Saskatchewan, with no mention of his part in Alberta's history. The same holds true for the second man to hold the job, Robert George Brett, 1915-25, who is in one of the stone mausoleums in the old cemetery in Banff, and for Dr. W. Egbert, 1925-31, and W.L. Walsh, 1931-36, both of whom are buried in Calgary's Union Cemetery.

Four are buried in Edmonton: P.C.H. Primrose, who served 1936 to 1937; J.C. Bowen, 1937 to 1950; J.J. Bowlen, 1950 to 1959; and J. Percy Page, 1959 to 1965. Only Bowen and Bowlen mention their service as lieutenant-governor. J. Percy Page doesn't even mention his record as coach of the famous Edmonton Grads basketball team, an even more surprising omission, some would feel.

The accomplishments of Ralph Steinhauer, the first native Albertan to hold the post of lieutenant-governor, are also left unsung. When I first saw his gravemarker, it was lying somewhat unceremoniously behind the undertaker's workshop in St. Paul, having been brought there to have Mrs. Steinhauer's name and dates added to it. Somewhere in the back of my mind I knew that every gravemarker had to be handled in a matter-of-fact way, but it was still a shock to find the former lieutenant-governor's marker lying amid a heap of lumber and unfinished granite markers. It has since been put back into its proper place in the United Church graveyard on the Saddle Lake Reserve.

Finally, there is Frank Lynch Staunton, who is buried in the foothills north of Cowley in the Livingstone Cemetery. He is the one man that I would have bet would NOT have mentioned the government appoint-ment, cowboys and ranchers being known for their disregard of titles and position. But at the bottom of his fairly modest marker are the words, **"Pioneer Rancher and Lieutenant Governor 1988-90."** Notice, how-ever, that "Pioneer Rancher" comes first in his list of accomplishments. We have to keep our priorities straight out here in the West.

~

I expected to find the words "Klondike" and "Gold Rush" liberally sprin-kled through our graveyards, especially in Edmonton. After all, the city celebrates Klondike Days every summer and admits that the gold rush gave its economy a very nice boost. But as so often happened in the course of my graveyard research, I was wrong. The words do show up here and there but not often. It's another story not told well in our grave-yards.

Goldseekers in the thousands from all over the world headed north in 1897 after hearing reports of "a ton of gold" found on Bonanza Creek in the Yukon. About 1,500 of them went north from Edmonton, which advertised itself as the "poor man's" entrance to the north. If you had any money at all, you tried to go by water, up the west coast to the rivers of the Yukon. But a lot of the guys looking for gold didn't have gold and therefore had to take the longer, more tortuous overland routes, either through the interior of British Columbia, or north from Edmonton. The overland routes look straightforward enough on the map, but none of them were, certainly not the one that wandered through the minefields of mud and muskeg, snow and cold north of Edmonton. It was so im-possible that most gold seekers gave up somewhere along the way and went home if they had any money left, or stayed where they were if they didn't. That's how the Peace River country got some of its very first pioneers, Klondike hopefuls who couldn't go one step further.

That may be why the gold rush doesn't figure prominently in our graveyards. It was the people who didn't make it who ended up living and dying in our midst, and even though they may have gone on to other important and worthwhile things, they may not have wanted to be re-minded of their first failure. It's one explanation anyway.

The one place that you can find mention of the Klondike is in the military section of certain graveyards. The police were a growth industry through those two crazy years because there was a tendency for goldseekers to put themselves above the law. A man who wouldn't dream of lying or cheating back home in Indiana would suddenly, as the fever hit him, lie and cheat and much worse, all in the name of gold. It could have been a hopelessly lawless time in Canadian history, but it wasn't, thanks to the North West Mounted Police.

So if you want to experience the Klondike, you'd better hie yourself to a military section of the graveyard or to the special sections set aside for NWMP and RCMP veterans. There you'll find gravemarkers like this one in the Calgary Union Cemetery.

In Memory of John J. Mahony
Feb. 10, 1879-April 24, 1944
Cpl. RNWMP Yukon Gold Rush 1898

One of the best stories about the Klondike is a story that involves beef on the hoof, not gold in the pan, but it too remains untold in the graveyard.

When I came across Billy Henry's unremarkable grave in the High River Cemetery and found no indication that he had been part of one of Alberta's best stories, I could have cried. There wasn't even an attempt to make us do our arithmetic and realize that Billy Henry had been 104 years old at his death in 1971 — as old as Canada was itself.

Billy Henry was born in Scotland in 1867. Half a planet away, a new country called Canada was just being carved out of whole cloth. The Henry family decided to take a chance on it and came to cowboy country around High River in 1885. It didn't take Billy long to make the adjustment: by 1898, he was such a capable cowhand that the meat-packer Pat Burns, who knew an opportunity when he saw one, hired him to take meat — on the hoof — to the Klondike. Over land and over sea, Billy Henry and his cowboys got 180 head of cattle to Dawson City. The adventure took eight long months. By the time the cattle got there, they were frozen meat. Even so, they were a welcome sight to prospectors who hadn't seen beef for months. No wonder Billy Henry found it hard to settle down to routine ranching after he got back. Not enough challenge.

In 1967, when Canada and Billy celebrated their centennials, High River put on the biggest birthday party ever, Calgary made him honorary parade marshall of the Stampede, and the Horseman's Hall of Fame named him among their number. When journalist Bruce Hutchison interviewed him in the midst of all the celebrations and asked him what made ranchers special, Billy answered simply, "They dreamed big."

That's what should have been on his gravemarker.

～

The farmers who pitched their lives in Alberta's backyard also dreamed big and planted dreams right along with the spring wheat. Always they hoped that this would be the big year, the year of big crops and big payments to the bank. It hardly ever happened that way — farming is too often the triumph of hope over experience — but farmers kept on hoping anyway and talking about "Next year."

Three men improved the odds considerably: Dr. William Harmon Fairfield, Asael Palmer, and Charles Sherwood Noble. They all made significant contributions to Alberta's most important industry, but none of their work is mentioned on their silent gravemarkers in the Lethbridge Mountainview Cemetery. Couldn't we give credit where credit is due?

Fairfield was associated with the Lethbridge Experimental Farm from 1905 to 1945. In that time, he did whatever he could to help farmers succeed at their task. He brought in improved seed, more specific fertilizers, new plant strains; he travelled all over to educate, advise, and demonstrate; always and everywhere he encouraged the planting of windbreaks and trees. In fact, if you happen to be standing in a southern Alberta cemetery right now, consider the caragana hedge. It's probably one of Fairfield's.

Asael Palmer also worked at the Lethbridge Experimental Farm, and like every other farmer in the south in the 1920s and 1930s, he watched with horror as their good black soil was blown to Kingdom Come or Saskatchewan, whichever came first. The soil drifting was a result of consecutive dry years plus farming methods that encouraged clean summer-fallowed fields. Observing that fields with leftover stubble didn't blow away, Palmer began experimenting with "trash covers" and eventually recommended them for all farmers in dry periods. It seems like a small thing — to encourage messy fields — but some historians credit Palmer with saving southern Alberta from becoming a complete dust bowl, useless for either crops or cattle.

There is no trash near his gravemarker, of course, but neither is there any indication of his important contribution to agriculture. Think how schoolchildren would come to a screeching halt in front of a gravemarker that paid tribute to Asael "Trash Cover" Palmer. They might even ask some questions and learn something.

Charles Sherwood Noble was into surface trash as well, only he went one step further and invented a special plow. Who says plows can only be invented in large industrial cities in other countries? Once he invented his Noble Blade, he set up a factory in Nobleford to manufacture it. The Noble Blade was constructed so that it cut up the soil beneath the surface, dealing death to weeds but leaving the surface unbroken so that the wind could not take away either the loose soil or the precious moisture stored beneath the surface.

In typical western Canadian fashion, Noble's grave doesn't tell any of this. It's just another great story left untold — and another illustration of how our gravemarkers often don't do justice to our history.

~

THE LAST WORD: I know that what does or does not go on a gravemarker is none of my business. And I'm sure that it was for the likes of me that Robert Emmet wrote the following epitaph back in 1803: **"Let there be no inscription upon my tomb; let no man write my epitaph; no man can write my epitaph."**

A slightly altered Emmet appears on the gravemarker of Will Kemna in Queen's Park Cemetery in Calgary. It says, **"Let no man write his epitaph."**

~

Stories on the Funny Side

Here lies the body of Solomon Pease
'Neath the daisies and the trees,
Pease is not here, only the pod,
Pease shelled out and went home to God.

...an epitaph reported by Emily Murphy of Edmonton

I wish I could make this chapter longer, but we western Canadians are not particularly funny in our graveyards. There has to be a reason for that, I'm sure. Maybe we're so new out here that we're not yet confident enough to joke about ourselves, especially in death. There are some amusing moments in graveyards in Great Britain and in certain parts of the United States. Even graveyards in eastern Canada generally contain a few lighthearted last words, but not out here. We take ourselves seriously from beginning to end; therefore, I didn't find the likes of the epitaph Emily Murphy reported in her 1910 book, *Janey Canuck in the West*. In fact, as I've been saying all along, I had a hard time finding words, period, on our gravemarkers; so it's no wonder I couldn't find many funny ones. If we say anything at all, it is more likely to be in the lugubrious vein like this epitaph in the Edmonton Cemetery on the tombstone of Henry Hardisty, who died in 1876:

Stop, Passenger, whilst passing by,
As you are now, so once was I.
As I am now, you too must be,
Oh, then prepare to follow me.

If that doesn't sober you up, I don't know what will!

About the only trace I could find of any levity surrounding death were the incidents that took place on the way to the graveyard, as was the case with the two undertakers who fought over the privilege of burying one another.

It all started with the death of a man near Red Deer. The man's daughter, who did not live in Red Deer, wired the local undertaker to meet the train on a certain day and look after her father's burial. So far, so good, except that the dead man's son did exactly the same thing. When the two discovered the duplication of orders, they decided to let them stand. After all, how could there be more than one undertaker in a town as small as Red Deer was in 1902? As it happens, there were two, Mr. Stone and Mr. Orme, and wouldn't you know it, each received one of the wires.

Messrs. Stone and Orme both turned up at the train station at the appointed time, and each tried to claim the body. The dispute over the body grew, and the two men decided finally to settle the matter with their fists. By this time, quite a crowd had gathered to witness the fight, the most excitement the town had seen for awhile. In the end, Mr. Stone won, settling once and for all just who would bury the deceased man; however, as he drove off, his rival Orme shook his fist and declared, "I'll have the pleasure of burying you yet."

But Orme just couldn't wait that long for revenge. The very next day, he charged Mr. Stone with assault, and Stone had to pay a fine for his part in the skirmish. As it turned out, Orme did have the pleasure of burying Stone. You might say that Stone's victory in the fistfight was a classic case of winning the battle but losing the war!

There is another story from the Red Deer area that still makes old-timers smile, although nobody seems to have any proof that it actually happened. It's one of those community stories that persists in spite of itself, the sort of thing that used to happen when people took church connections very seriously.

The Anglican Church at Pine Lake looks too innocent to be the source of any kind of community dissent. It's a white frame church with all the traditional touches — a red turret and roof, a bell tower, a scattering of graves all around the church. It has a British look to it, even the hills around the lake are more rounded and polite than most western Canadian hills. Indeed, the church came about because two maiden aunts in England didn't want their nephews on the frontier of Canada to turn into godless heathens; so they donated money to have the Holy Trinity Anglican Church built.

When the money first arrived, the Alford brothers — Reg, Bert, and Henry — thought it was for them personally. They were dreaming dreams of a hot time in the old town when they turned the page and read, "We are deeply concerned to think that you boys have no opportunity to attend divine worship, so we are sending the money to form the nucleus of a fund for building a church in your community."

The church was built, but the community didn't always live up to the ideals that the aunties in England had hoped to put in place. Old-timers tell the story of the farmer who up and died. He had been an Anglican, so he should have been accepted into the graveyard without question, but there had been some disagreement. Nobody can remember what the rift was about, but eventually a compromise was worked out. The church fathers would allow the coffin to be buried in the graveyard as long as it was placed close to the church door. Since they were quite sure the old farmer couldn't afford a marker of any sort, they expected the area would soon revert to a path again, as if nothing and no one had happened.

When some of the farmer's buddies heard that version of the story, they were so incensed that they bought the biggest marker they could afford and mounted it at the head of their friend's last resting place. From then on, church faithfuls had to walk around the big marker, remembering every time they did so that they had demonstrated a meanness of spirit in denying their old neighbour his rightful place.

When I checked in 1991, there was no gravemarker on a path leading into the church, and I almost decided I'd have to give up the story. Then someone told me that the entrances and exits had been changed over the years. Could it be that the old farmer got his revenge twice, first when they had to walk around him and then when they had to change the doors? I hope so.

~

The coal mining town of Bankhead in the Rockies was a model town. The Canadian Pacific Railway built the town in 1904 and put in one of everything — one school, one barbershop, one church, one butcher shop, etc. — but they did not include one graveyard. You have to think that they didn't expect anyone to die, because this was a town that was planned down to the last detail. Miners were to live on the same street as mine owners, Italians next to Poles, Catholics next to Protestants. Everyone was to have an equal place in this utopia, and everybody was to be nice to everyone else — except for the Chinese workers who lived in awful shanties behind the slack heaps from the mine; it was not required to be nice to them.

Even the best of all possible worlds experiences death, and that's what happened in Bankhead occasionally. Because Bankhead didn't have its own graveyard, people who died in Bankhead were buried in Banff, and the reception after the funeral was held in Banff as well. Those Bankhead folks must have known how to throw a good wake, since Banff residents complained about the rowdiness of the Bankhead bashes. Wreck your own town, they suggested, so a cemetery was finally carved out of the hillside above the town. The trouble was that everyone was superstitious. No one wanted their loved one to be the first to be buried in the cemetery for fear other family members would follow. The taboo was not broken until one of the Chinese men was buried there in 1921.

The following year, the town itself died. Markets for coal dried up, it was the wrong kind of coal, the miners kept striking for better wages and working conditions, the national park decided they didn't want a mine inside park limits after all, and so on. What with such a multitude of problems, the CPR had to admit defeat and move the town out of the park, leaving nothing behind but a lot of concrete foundations and one lonesome grave in the graveyard.

Even that grave did not remain. Seven years later, the Chinese man's body was disinterred and shipped back to China to be with his ancestors. Bankhead, it would appear, was not meant for burying.

~

The Fort Smith story isn't exactly a knee slapper either, but it does offer some very funny twists. Once upon a time, as near as anyone can figure, Edward Martin came to the most northerly part of Alberta and established himself as a woodcutter for the Hudson's Bay Company. Through the long, cold winters, he would haul fallen timbers over the snow to the edge of the Slave River. There he would cut them into the lengths specified by the HBC and pile them by the river, awaiting pickup through the summer for the steamboats that plied the river. Each pile had to be 4x4x8 feet, but Edward Martin always added a few extra logs, just to be sure. That's why he became known up and down the river as the man who made honest piles.

In the summer, he would retreat to the back country and stay out of sight. He was known only by his trademark neat piles. But one fall, he didn't come out; his wood piles didn't appear in their usual place. When the authorities went looking for him, they discovered him in his tiny shack in the bush, dead from a self-inflicted bullet wound. There wasn't much in the way of personal effects — no identification other than pay envelopes, no last will and testament — but there was some money. A judge somewhere along the line decided that some of the money might as well be used for a memorial. A concrete monument weighing some 3,500 pounds was shipped by rail and steamer from Edmonton — perhaps using enroute some of the logs that Edward Martin had so carefully piled in winters past — to Fort Smith, where it was erected exactly on the border of Alberta and the Northwest Territories.

There it stands to this day, a rather beat up looking concrete tree trunk on top of a concrete pile of logs. The inscription, the best part of the whole story, says:

To the memory of Edward Martin, died June 13, 1928
The best woodcutter of the north,
He supplied fuel to steamboats.
A silent and lone man who took pride in his work
And built an honest pile.

If the story had ended there, it would have been one of those bittersweet tales of a man who craved privacy above everything else, yet ended up as a tourist attraction. But there is more to it than that. A year or two later, a woman turned up in Fort Smith and demanded the money that Martin had left behind. She was his sister, she said, and she was entitled to the money, even the part that had been spent on the memorial.

Then, according to yet another postscript, another woman turned up, this one claiming to be his wife. I don't know if she got anything or proved anything or even if she existed. This is one of those lovely stories that improves with age. Who's to say what is true anymore? Which is why I've decided that Edward Martin probably had good reason to high tail it into the bush: he seems to have known some pretty formidable women.

Nevertheless, the marker remains, the only tribute that I know of to an "honest pile."

~

You could never have accused Baldy Red of honesty. Mind you, you couldn't have accused him of dishonesty either, since he always had an answer ready for any occasion. Once when a cow he did not own ended up on the end of a rope in his yard, he said, "I don't know how that happened. This is my rope but I don't know how the cow got attached to it."

No wonder the north country waited for the next installment of any Baldy Red adventures. He was irrepressible, and the Hythe Cemetery has recognized that fact by installing a storyboard that outlines some of his better escapades. It's the only time I've found storyboards in a rural cemetery, but it seems to me to be a good idea. There are three altogether in Hythe's cemetery — one for Baldy Red, one for Dora "Ma" Brainard, who ran a stopping house along the Alaska Highway and was famous for her chicken dinners, and one for Kelly Sunderman, who was a freighter and surveyor and founder of the town of Hythe. Taken together, the storyboards tell something of the story of transportation in that difficult country so many years ago.

"Baldy Red" made people laugh, which is why he got his own storyboard in the cemetery even though he was something of a scoundrel. His real name was George Yeomans, and he was a freight hauler. Most of the time he hauled the usual stuff — household goods, groceries, supplies — but every now and then he yielded to temptation and added liquor to his load. At the turn of the century, liquor was illegal in the North.

The North West Mounted Police did their best to stop the illicit traffic; they checked the loads of most freighters and kept an eye on known carriers like Baldy. At first he used the usual tricks, such as hiding the booze in coal oil cans or medicine bottles. Then he tried to avoid check points by driving down the Whiskey Trail, a trail that the police weren't supposed to know about but soon did. Whether Baldy resorted to the tree trick is not known, but he likely did whatever worked. In the tree trick, carriers tied bottles to a tree trunk and floated them down a river, past the police, then picked them up later when the river took a turn.

Some of Baldy's best tricks involved the clergy. On one occasion, he was overtaken on the Edson Trail by a Grande Prairie minister. As the minister drove his skittish team past Baldy, he admitted that he wasn't too good at controlling horses. Souls maybe, but not horses. As quick as you could say Amen, Baldy offered to trade outfits. He would drive the minister's team and buggy to Grande Prairie for him, and the minister could drive his more experienced, plodding, manageable horses. What a nice guy. When they got closer to Grande Prairie, the police gave Baldy's rig a good going-over but waved the minister and his load through.

Another time, Baldy offered a ride to two Catholic nuns. He re-arranged his cargo, a lot of which had a tendency to gurgle, and covered it with buffalo robes. Then he seated the good Sisters upon it, and just to be sure they were comfortable and warm, he covered them and the load with more buffalo robes. Such a gentleman. When the Mounties rode up for their customary search, they saw the nuns sitting there, as sweet as pie, and what could they do but wave Baldy on? They may have had their suspicions, but the Sisters never did. They were enormously grateful for Baldy's kindness during the long trip. He was delighted with the whole episode, having outwitted the police and received the church's blessing all in one fell swoop.

By the time Baldy died at age sixty-nine in 1936, the heyday of the freight hauler was over. Trains had arrived in the Peace country; the automobile was making inroads. Liquor had gone respectable too, available wherever a government outlet existed. It just wasn't as much fun anymore. And for Baldy Red, the game was everything.

≈

For a while the editor of the *Innisfail Province* labelled Births, Marriages and Deaths under the headings of "Hatched, Matched and Dispatched." That sort of levity would never last in today's politically correct environment. Someone would surely be offended. Nor would the local band get away with playing "Silver Threads Among the Gold" at a funeral, even if it was the most solemn thing they had in their repertoire.

≈

The "grave diviner" in this story was brought into the picture for entirely serious reasons, but even if the story is not funny as such, it is unusual. We don't have a lot of people who, with divining rods and lengths of wire, go out into graveyards looking for unmarked graves, but that's what happened in Seven Persons.

The cemetery in any community is usually just there. It's part of the scenery, filled occasionally with people and cars so that passersby know that a death has occurred. A mound of newly dug soil will scar the grounds for a short time, then the grass grows over it and life goes on. Now and then, though, the graveyard moves unexpectedly into the front row of community concerns. Suddenly people are mad at city hall or mad at one another, and it turns into a nasty confrontation. Cemeteries are not a rational matter that can be administered by organizational flow charts and economic projections. Just ask the good persons of Seven Persons south of Medicine Hat. They woke up one summer day in 1980 to discover that the Municipal District was thinking of selling a piece of land by the cemetery to the farmer who had been using it for years as part of his irrigation system. Not only that, but someone's cows had been getting into the cemetery. Something in the community snapped; the cemetery had been ignored long enough. The Seven Persons Historical Society was formed and battle lines drawn.

The Society argued that cemetery boundaries should be extended to include the piece of land in question because there were bodies buried out there without markers. When the municipal authorities asked for proof, Society members went up to Edmonton to consult the Vital Statistics Branch. According to those records, there had been some fifty-nine burials in the Seven Persons Cemetery, only about ten of which were marked, so some of those bodies could very well have been in the larger area. Besides, old-timers said they were there, and they should know.

Furthermore — and this was the Historical Society's coup — Lez Philpott said there were at least thirty bodies outside the fenced part of the graveyard, and he should know. Philpott was southern Alberta's grave diviner, and if anyone could find hidden graves, he could. With his chrome divining rods and wire antennae, he paced the whole area, stopping to mark the spots that caused his rods to bend. When he was finished, there were markers scattered all over the larger area.

The manager of the Municipal District said a diviner's evidence was dubious at best. In any case, the markers disappeared within the next few weeks, so even the dubious evidence was gone. This was not a friendly fight, and even ten years later, one of the original members of the Historical Society was writing to a local paper saying that "We pray for long lives and another election." In other words, they were still mad at both the local and provincial government.

It was the Municipal District's turn to apply science to the problem. They sent in a grader and an archaeologist. The grader stripped the topsoil; the archeologist looked for signs of burial sites but found none. Then the archaeologist took out his auger and probed deeper in several sites, at one point finding signs of wood on the tool when it was brought to the surface. That could certainly have indicated a coffin, but it wasn't technically within the disputed area. So the archaeologist wasn't a great help either, on top of which some members of the Historical Society claimed that probes and augers and the like constituted desecration, and they were ready to sue.

In the end, a compromise was effected that didn't really suit either side. The MD retained ownership of the land, the farmer was given the privilege of running his irrigation pivot across it, and the Historical Society got a government grant to erect a cairn within the cemetery in memory of those who are buried there. The handsome cairn is now the best part. The graveyard itself is no great beauty; I rather expected more after reading about all its troubles. But the cairn lists names and dates, and ends with the information that an unidentified man drowned in the dam in 1925, and a sheepherder, also unnamed, died in a blizzard in 1927. These and many more nameless persons may be buried in the Seven Persons Cemetery.

Ask the MD authorities and they'll tell you that graveyards are a living example of the power of passion over reason. Which is probably why I haven't found many funny stories in our graveyards. We feel too deeply about the people who have gone before.

~

Cookies are about as cheerful as we get about funerals and graveyards in this part of the country. These ones got their name from the fact they can be made quickly without any baking necessary. Thus, if a homemaker had to produce a contribution for the funeral or wanted to take some baking to the home of the bereaved, she could always whip up a batch of Funeral Cookies. They taste just as good without the name — in our family, they're known as Ada's Chocolate Unbaked Cookies — but the original name is another good reminder of the way we were.

Funeral Cookies

2 cups white sugar
1/2 cup butter or margarine
1/2 cup milk
1 tsp. vanilla
1/2 tsp. salt
3 cups rolled oats
1/2 cup cocoa
1 cup unsweetened short grain coconut

Put first three ingredients into a heavy pot and bring to a rolling boil, stirring all the while. Remove from heat. Stir in remaining ingredients and drop by spoonsful on wax paper to cool. Do this quickly so that you can get the cookies formed before the batter begins to get hard in the pot. If some of it gets hard in the pot, let it cool and then give to the kids to lick. Take the nicely formed shiny ones to the funeral. Keep the ragged ones for the family. They taste fine.

∽

THE LAST WORD: I despaired of finding this epitaph in western Canada but another graveyard enthusiast found it in the Okotoks Cemetery and passed it along. It's called "The Tired Woman's Epitaph" and it's just about as funny as we get. It appears on the gravemarker of Harriet Elizabeth Connell, 1898-1989.

Weep not for me now,
Weep not for me never.
For I'm going to do nothing
For ever and ever.

∽

Stories of Immigration
and Settlement

Make no small plans....
They hold no magic to stir men's blood.

...from the gravemarker of Senator Donald Cameron
and his wife, Mary, in the Banff Cemetery

Over and over again, our graveyards tell the story of big plans. They
don't always tell such stories directly — our western modesty keeps getting in the way — but there are enough hints to put together the larger
story. Take, for example, the simple, straightforward gravemarker in the
Marwayne Cemetery that says, "In memory of W.C. Marfleet who established the first Marwayne post office in 1906." I don't know one other
thing about Mr. Marfleet, but I do know that a mere ninety years ago in
this province, Marwayne didn't have a post office. The people who lived
there didn't have newspapers and regular mail from home, wherever home
was. And that's the other thing that the gravemarker underlines — that
most of us in the West came from somewhere else. We came from other
countries to make a new start; we came with big plans and little else.
That most of us managed to survive, and thrive even, is an amazing story,
and our graveyards do their part in telling that story.

Sometimes the story of big plans is told or hinted at with the word
"first," as it is with Marfleet. In the Edmonton Cemetery is the
gravemarker of Matthew McCauley, 1850-1930, who has to get the award
for the most firsts mentioned on one gravemarker: "**First Mayor of Edmonton, Member of First Alberta Legislature, Chairman of First Edmonton School Board**." Other than telling us that McCauley was into
most everything in the earliest days of Edmonton, the words also say
clearly that Edmonton is rather young, as cities go; so is the province of
Alberta, for that matter; and as for formal education, it too is a recent
development in Canada's West. Otherwise, how could a man who lived
in this century be involved in so many "firsts?"

Mind you, the world has changed considerably since he enjoyed all his "firsts." I checked up on Mr. McCauley, and it turns out he'd likely be run out of town nowadays. He was on the impatient side, to put it mildly. When town officials dithered about an unsightly shack on the edge of a friend's property, McCauley took matters into his own hands and pushed the thing over the river bank. Problem solved. That would not be allowed nowadays, even if you were the "first."

Andrew Sibbald's gravemarker in the Morley Cemetery across the road from the McDougall United Church states that Mr. Sibbald was **"The First Schoolteacher in the West."** It's another claim that speaks of our beginnings and the big plans we had. Mr. Sibbald set up a school because there were more and more settlers in the country wanting formal education for their children, and because he and the missionary McDougalls wanted to offer education to the Indian children in the area. It was their Christian duty to do so. That his contribution would now be questioned — and his claim to be "first" denied — would surprise him enormously. He was only doing what he had been taught was right.

In the graveyard next to St. Mary's Romanian Orthodox Church of Boian near Willingdon are two gravemarkers concerned with "firsts." Ioan T. Toma's gravemarker says, **"Elected First Trustee, January 20, 1901, to acquire land and to organize the building of the church".** Next to him is Veronica Toma's tombstone, which tells us that she was **"Elected First President of Sisters of the Orthodox Church of Boian, 1936."** In other words, the Tomas were pillars of the little church that presides over the cemetery. That's why I like finding markers like that. They tell me something about the community, and even if their claims might be challenged, they still help fill in the blanks. Even the fact that history gets rewritten is part of the story.

Other interesting "firsts" that were established in this brave new country have been left off our gravestones, much to the dismay of certain historians and friends of the deceased. For instance, in northern Alberta, there's a movement afoot to mark the grave of Allie Brick with more pomp and ceremony. Allie Brick was the first MLA from the Peace River district, and when he drove down to Edmonton for the very first sitting of the new legislative assembly, he arrived with several freight teams. That in itself was nothing unusual; Edmontonians were used to seeing long freight teams and wagons proceeding down Jasper Avenue. What they weren't used to was the sight of two moose prancing along behind the wagons. Allie Brick's pet moose couldn't see why they shouldn't be included, so they came along.

Of course, none of this is recorded on Brick's terribly quiet grave in Keg River, and probably it won't be. If I had my way, I'd see to it that Allie Brick was remembered as the first and likely the last Alberta politician to bring his four-legged supporters to the legislature.

$$\sim$$

Do you want to know how the West was won? Never mind all the scholarly tomes that have been produced on the subject, just go to the United Church of Christ graveyard at Josephburg, twenty-five miles northeast of Edmonton. There, under huge spruce trees, I found a homemade concrete pedestal, leaning just a bit, bearing the message in German that "**Here lie Jakob and Elizabeth Thomas**." It was not the grandeur of the marker that struck me; it was the simple, direct message, obviously put there by hand. I couldn't get the image out of my mind, so the next time I was in the Calgary Public Library, I looked up the Thomas family in the Josephburg local history book. It didn't take me long to realize that they illustrated very well just how western Canada came to be settled and populated.

They came for the usual reasons — they wanted land and a future for themselves and their children, so they packed up their home in Josefburg in the Galicia district of Austria/Germany, and they moved to Canada. They ended up in Dunmore, on the dry land around Medicine Hat. Two years and two summers of drought later, they decided to move one more time. Advance scouts had checked out the area around Edmonton and found it to be more like the land they knew in Austria. Some fifty-three families hit the road again. They separated at Edmonton. Some went to Fort Saskatchewan, some to Stony Plain, and some to the Leduc area. Nine families moved to what is now called Josephburg, and by that fall, all nine families had homes and a beginning in the new country.

Back in Germany, the news travelled quickly that Alberta was a good place if you could work hard. By 1900, German immigrants accounted for the third largest ethnic group in the province, and what with additional immigration and large families, that percentage climbed until Germans were the second largest ethnic group for awhile. By 1911, for example, there was not one single quarter-section of land in Josephburg that was not owned by an original pioneer or one of their descendants.

As for the Thomas family, listen to this arithmetic. They came with three children. Those three children grew up and had a total of twenty-four children, and that's how the West was won.

~

In 1899, in the district of Bukowina in the brave old world known as the Austro-Hungarian Empire lived six Shandro brothers. When they heard the incredible news that a country called Canada wanted settlers and was practically giving away good farm land, they could hardly believe their good fortune. A total of 160 acres for $10. Whoever heard of such a thing? They knew they had to move fast. So the three eldest Shandro sons sold their share of the family lands to the three younger ones, and in March of 1899, they set out, a total of twenty-eight men, women and children. None of them spoke English, none of them had the money to pay for much more than the land. Once they got that land, it had to provide. Land was the magic word, which is why they made sure to pack a sharp spade to dig and find the best soil possible when they got to Canada. They knew their soil even if they didn't know this new country.

It was exactly what Clifford Sifton had predicted back in Ottawa when he came up with the idea of advertising in eastern Europe for immigrants to fill up western Canada. The men in sheepskin coats know how to work, he said, and they value land. They'll make the West grow. Clifford Sifton was the Minister of the Interior for the Laurier government in Ottawa, and he was right.

The Shandro party travelled halfway around the world, and by May they were travelling east of Edmonton, looking for their Valhalla. The spade was kept busy, but it wasn't until they were about 100 miles out of Edmonton that they decided to stop. The soil was good, there was water available, there was no shortage of trees, it was rolling parkland like home. This would be it.

The area eventually became known as the Shandro area, and a town that became Willingdon grew nearby, but that day when twenty-eight people from Bukowina stopped, it was simply The Place To Stop, The Place To Start. Three weeks later, Anna Shandro gave birth to a baby boy, John. The community now numbered twenty-nine.

That first summer, when there must have been a thousand things to do, Anastasia and Stefan Shandro took a walk one day with other members of the community and found a place for a church. They selected a spot on top of a hill that looked over their new homes, their new lives. Anastasia took two willow branches, tied them together to form a cross, and put the cross into the ground to mark the site. Several years later, the Shandro St. Mary's Russo-Greek Orthodox Church was consecrated, its shining domes a reminder of the old country.

In 1988, not quite 100 years later, the forty-two grandchildren of Stefan and Anastasia got together to pay special tribute to their grandparents, as a result of which there's a big new granite gravemarker in the Shandro graveyard "In Loving Memory" of those who led the way.

$\sim$

As these settlers from all over the world moved into Alberta, different versions of God moved in as well, each version requiring its own church and graveyard. Thus, one community might have an Anglican church and graveyard, a Presbyterian one, a Roman Catholic one, and an Eastern Orthodox one. Sometimes all religions and denominations were expected to use a community graveyard, in which case they put up fences or in some way delineated the differences. Once when I asked a local man why his community had so many small graveyards, he told me, "In them days, they had their differences."

There aren't so many differences now, but you can still spot the original arrangements, especially in the case of Eastern Orthodox graveyards, which are marked by the white rounded crosses or Eastern Orthodox crosses. The graveyards themselves are quite distinctive, particularly the very earliest ones, and they are quite beautiful, especially if you're lucky enough to see one in the fog. The morning I was at St. Mary's Russian Greek Orthodox west of Nisku, everything was blanketed by fog, the church just a ghost behind the trees.

To the west of the church, barely visible in the mist, I found the graveyard. The front rows were filled with the oldest graves, and as I approached through the fog, I could have been in the old country. The graves were mostly marked with either of the traditional crosses and most had additional decoration — flowers carved into the hard surface, photographs of the deceased above their names, depictions of Christ on the cross. Many also had silk or plastic flowers arranged on the ground beside them or actually wired to the tombstone. The inscriptions were written in the Cyrillic script.

But I didn't have to go down many more rows before things began to change. The markers had less decoration on them or none at all; there were fewer crosses and more plain black granite markers, the Cyrillic script was replaced by English. Apparently it didn't take very many years for some of the eastern European settlers to change their ways, to become like other Canadians not only in life but in death.

I experienced the same sort of cultural progression when I visited Spedden, population sixty-six. The man at the service station thought I was absolutely mad when I asked him if there were any graveyards nearby. "How many you want?" he asked in amazement. He knew of at least four within a ten-mile radius of Spedden, he told me, but there might be more. After all, he had only lived there all his life, some fifty years. His father was the person to ask, he said.

I said four would be fine, thanks, so he wiped his hands on his coveralls and drew me a map, and for the rest of that sunny afternoon, I found clues to the story of Spedden. The first graveyard on my map, a tangle of weeds and bush abandoned since the 1930s, spoke of the very first settlers who came into the area, the ones who had so little that they had to bury their people under wooden crosses that are now rotting away, or homemade concrete crosses pitted by time and weather now. It would have been quite grand in its day, as grand as anything could be that was made with love, not money. The irises would have been grand too; they still bloomed here and there in the midst of the weeds and bush. In memory of whom? I wondered. Even the straggly caragana hedge spoke of people who made the most of very little. Caragana was easy to get in the early days; it grew without fuss; it would have to do.

The second graveyard spoke about transitions. From a distance, the traditional white crosses on top of the hill were incredibly beautiful, etched against the summer sky and surrounded by brilliant pink and yellow flowers. Seen from close up, it was plain that many of them needed a paint job, the silk flowers on the columns needed changing. The new black granite markers further down the hill weren't nearly as beautiful, but they didn't need painting either, and there were no arrangements of silk flowers. The world is changing in the graveyard just as it is in society generally. The women who used to keep up the cemetery are working outside the home now; they don't have time. The men who used to mow and weed and plant caragana hedges are doing other things. The graveyard sometimes suffers.

Spedden #3 was different again, sombre somehow, dominated by an iron cross with a figure of the suffering Christ on it. It seemed to say that life was harsh and then you died, and that's how it was for many of the eastern European settlers who came to Canada with nothing but their lives. Why shouldn't the graveyard tell us that?

The fourth and final graveyard, the newest one in the community, tells the story of conformity and assimilation. Other than the occasional words in Russian, the gravemarkers look like those in any other part of North America.

~

Eastern Europeans came to Canada for land and a future, but Rev. Halvor Nilsen Ronning established a Norwegian settlement in the north Peace River country because of "The Lord." Ronning feared that if his fellow Norwegians became scattered and separated from their church life in this new country of Canada, they would neglect their religious duties. So he came up with the idea of establishing a colony that would be both Norwegian and religious. A fairly logical decision, some would say; others would say an impossible dream, but not Rev. Ronning. This is what he said: "As Abraham was commanded to get out of his country and go unto a land the Lord would show him, so sounded in my heart an inner call to me."

Even though he was in his fifties and had already served the Lord as a missionary in China for seventeen years, Rev. Ronning set out to see just where he was called to go next. Part of his trip involved travelling over the infamous Edson Trail from Edson to the Grande Prairie area in 1912, a trial for the godly and ungodly alike. Ronning wrote later:

> We met several people who had turned back. They told us that
> their wagons had broken down and some of their horses had
> died. They advised us against going any further. It was hard on
> faith and patience but my many experiences in China stood me
> in good stead.

Two weeks later, he found the promised land.

At sunset we reached our destination. On a fine open plain we rested about an hour. The land here consisted of wide, sweeping slopes; the whole landscape looking like an immense park. The grass was abundant. There was running water and a fine piece of timberland nearby. Small wonder that we called it Valhalla, the home of the gods.

Indeed, Ronning had found good land. The Valhalla area near Grande Prairie is renowned for its good crops and gardens, as well as for its upstanding citizens, most of whom are descended from or were influenced by the Lutherans who followed Ronning to this place.

After finding his Valhalla, Ronning returned to Camrose to make arrangements for the move. In March of the next year, the expedition set forth with four teams and wagons, Mrs. Ronning and five of the couple's children, three cows, two turkeys, two geese, a piano, a stove, two beds, and a rocking chair. Two older sons, Nelius and Chester, walked in later.

Maybe it was the challenge of that long and difficult walk; most certainly it had something to do with the fact that his youth was spent in China; maybe it was a little bit of his father's devotion to God and duty, but young Chester Ronning went on to several very distinguished careers. After serving as principal of the Camrose Lutheran College for years, he entered provincial politics, then served in various capacities with the Department of External Affairs in Ottawa, specializing always in the Far East.

For once, Rev. Ronning stayed closer to home, living out the rest of his years in Valhalla. The graveyard where he is buried is unique in that it's full of Scandinavian names, but it also features a stone cairn that honours the people who died in the two world wars as well as the men and women who pioneered in the Valhalla area. It's the only tribute I have seen that puts the two kinds of war together — the war fought on battlegrounds, the war fought on frontiers — but I sense the influence of Rev. Ronning. I think he would argue that all lives and all deaths have significance, and for that, he would say, we have to thank the Lord.

~

A dream of a different sort brought about Amber Valley, the community east of Athabasca that was settled between 1910 and 1920 by Blacks from the southern United States. It was a pocket of settlement quite unlike any other in Alberta, and when I began my graveyard research, I was anxious to find the Amber Valley graveyard. Would it give any clues to the unique nature of the community?

As it turned out, the first challenge was finding Amber Valley itself. There's no town as such anymore, but there are signs to the district of Amber Valley on highway 2 as you approach Athabasca from the south. As for locating the graveyard, that's an even bigger challenge. We asked a friendly farmer for directions, and even though he pointed right at the piece of bush where the graveyard is located, we still had to back-track four times. We finally found it where he said it was, "just past the granaries where the fields bend," at the end of a barely noticeable path through tall grass.

It's a wild patch of growth now, with graves scattered willy-nilly among the wild rose bushes and weeds, and as hard as I looked, I couldn't find anything that said definitively, "This place was different from most." Only the names on several graves hinted at differences. For instance, almost lost in a tangle of grass was the marker of Missouri Mapp, 1886-1921. "Missouri" as a first name is not that common in western Canada. Nor is "Jefferson," the first name on a nearby marker for Jefferson Davis Edwards and his wife Martha, but beyond that, the Amber Valley graveyard told the same stories as most western Canadian graveyards, or at least hinted at them. On the back of the Edwards marker, for example, were the words: **"Moving spirit of the pioneer group which developed the Amber Valley district."**

In 1910, Jefferson and Martha Edwards boarded a train in Tulsa, Oklahoma, bound for Edmonton, Alberta, wherever that was. They were two of the approximately 1,000 Black immigrants who moved to western Canada between 1910 and 1920. Even though American citizens had been welcomed into Canada as immigrants for years, this sudden appearance of Black Americans caught western Canadians off guard. Some covered their surprise and opposition with nice words, saying things like the Canadian climate is too tough "for people whose native land is in tropical regions." That's how an Edmonton immigration agent put it. Others didn't bother with the niceties and actually circulated a petition in Edmonton stating that, "It is a matter of common knowledge that it has been proved in the United States that negroes and whites cannot live in proximity without the occurrence of revolting lawlessness and the development of bitter race hatred." But because the Black immigrants promptly disappeared into remote regions in northern Alberta, most of the rhetoric died down.

Other Black immigrants went to the nearby towns of Wildwood, Campsie, Barrhead, and Breton, but only Amber Valley was exclusively Black at the beginning. At its peak in the 1930s, there were some 350 Blacks living there, about 95 per cent of the population.

For a while, life was grand. The soil wasn't great, but the company and the freedom were. The settlers started a school, then a church, then an annual picnic that became so popular it went on for three days and attracted people from miles around. According to Jefferson Edwards, one of the organizers, "We had races — horse races, riding steer. There'd be boxing, wrestling, everything you could think of. People wouldn't go home. They'd wait around that schoolhouse for the next day of the picnic."

But the same conditions that made it work for them in the beginning worked against them in the end — the isolation, the scarcity of jobs, the limited land available, and so on. The original idea of living together, each family on a quarter-section, was fine in the early days, but as families grew and sons and daughters needed land of their own, younger generations had to move away. Some of the settlers drifted back south, and gradually the community lost its all-Black character.

Besides, it had to be admitted that the country was colder than what they were used to. Martha Edwards said that she and Jefferson spent their first winter in a log house "that you could throw a cat through the cracks." The Canadian North was a long way from the American South in more ways than one!

~

It was Canada's cold that forced Wong Yet to begin the process of adjustment to a new country. It was that or stay frozen to the wall.

Many Chinese immigrants first came to Canada to help build the railway. That was their ticket, they hoped, to a new life in Canada. If they were lucky, they lived through the ordeal, but a great many died during the construction because the Chinese people were considered less than human and forced to live in perfectly awful conditions. One estimate claims that more than four Chinese workers died for every mile of constructed railway. In the Crowsnest Pass, people can remember seeing Chinese graves along the railroad tracks, just bumps of earth labelled Chinaman #1, Chinaman #2 and so on.

After the railway was finished, some of the workers returned to China; some went to the west coast because of the climate and the company of other Chinese expatriates; a few ventured into the small towns of Alberta. Not all of the Chinese immigrants to Canada came as a result of the railway, of course. Some came later, looking for adventure and opportunity in "The Land of the Golden Mountain." Things didn't look all that golden — or rosy either — in 1898, when Wong Yet set up a laundry in the settlement that would become Olds. His tar paper shack was so cold that his traditional Chinese pigtail, his queue, froze to the wall while he slept. What could he do but cut off the queue and carry on? Gradually he learned the language and some of the customs, and by 1903, he had enough money to send for his only son, Wong Pond. Together they added a restaurant to the laundry, thus providing the two services that Canadian communities allowed the Chinese in those days: cleaning and cooking.

In 1922, Wong Pond brought his son Frank from China, and the three of them added a pool hall and theatre to their string of businesses. Frank was the first generation to pick a wife in Canada. He married Irene Won, and their five children all graduated from high school in Olds, all of them thoroughly modern Canadians. Son Stewart still lives in Olds and, with his dad, supervises The Public Lunch, still the unofficial meeting place for town and country folk in the Olds area.

When Wong Yet died, his body was sent back to China to be buried. It was the choice of most of the first generation Chinese immigrants to go back to the old country. But the second generation, Wong Pond and his wife, broke with tradition and are buried in the Olds Cemetery under a stone that looks a lot like every other gravemarker in the place.

It took that family exactly one generation to make the transition.

~

On a warm April afternoon, I visited the old Chinese cemetery in Calgary because I had been told that April is one of three months that Chinese people observe special traditions at the graves of their ancestors, the others being July and September. Sure enough, the graveyard was filled with signs of recent ceremonies. For one thing, I found empty ketchup cans everywhere — the large, restaurant-size cans. It seems the cans are ideal for holding joss sticks, the sticks of incense that are burned as part of the remembrance ceremonies. Many of the graves also had fresh flowers or live plants arranged around them, while others had food placed nearby — apples, oranges, egg shells, raw potatoes, buns.

A young couple arrived with plastic containers full of the materials they needed. The man put the joss sticks into the can first and lit them, then he broke the boiled eggs and scattered the shells. His wife arranged apples and oranges at the base of the grave, put fresh flowers into a vase and tried to anchor it against the wind. She attempted to put several small, rectangular pieces of paper on top of the marker, but she couldn't find enough rocks to hold them down. Eventually she had to put them under the oranges on the ground. Neither said a word while all of this was going on. Then they washed their hands in water from yet another plastic container, dried them on a paper towel, and headed back to their car. On the way out, they passed the pagoda-like building at the entrance to the graveyard, the building that some call the worshipping pavilion. Offerings of fruit, flowers, and joss sticks had been left there as well.

I was told later that it's all part of age-old traditions that modern Chinese Canadians don't really understand but observe anyway out of respect for those who came before. After all, those originals worked so hard to make their dreams happen, to ensure a good life for those who now visit the graveyard.

~

THE LAST WORD: The people who made new beginnings in this country generally came for the same reason: to make a better life for themselves and their children. Nowhere is that stated quite so clearly as on the gravemarker of Jose Chua Ma, 1912-90, in the Rockyview Garden of Peace, east of Calgary.

I Have A Dream To See My Children
Clad better Than I
Educated More Than I
And In a Society Better Than Mine

~

Stories on the Gruesome Side

Here Rests His Heart

...epitaph on the gravemarker for Father Albert
Lacombe's heart, which is buried in Calgary

Gruesome may be too strong a word to use to describe the stories that
follow, but in the course of my graveyard research, I did occasionally
find a piece of history that veered in that direction. Certainly that was
the case with the rather bizarre tale of John Rowand, a story I first
encountered in one of Emily Murphy's books. As soon as I read her
version of the story, which sounded for all the world like a Grimm's fairy
tale, I knew I had to find out more.

John Rowand was a Hudson's Bay factor back in the days when to
have that job in western Canada was to be king of a very large piece of
land. The work suited him just fine; there was no doubt that he enjoyed
power and authority. He even had a castle built for his family in Fort
Edmonton, a three-storey effort that looked entirely out of place among
the small log shacks and tipis where his men lived. It was dubbed
"Rowand's Folly," but he didn't care. Why should he? He was the boss.

Because he worked as hard or harder than his men, Fort Edmonton
was a model of accomplishment and efficiency — roads were carved out
of the bush, boats were built to use on the rivers, gardens were planted,
meat supplies maintained, horses tended. It was no wonder that George
Simpson, Rowand's boss at HBC headquarters, pretty well left Rowand
alone. After all, he was doing a good job, in spite of the occasional complaint about his autocratic style of management. Simpson brushed off
the complaints, explaining that Rowand was, "Of a fiery disposition and
bold as a Lion."

A "grand little man" was what Roman Catholic missionary Father
Albert Lacombe called him. But he did get after him on one occasion for
mistreating one of his boatmen. "Can't you let him rest?" Father Lacombe
asked. "He's been sick." Rowand would have none of that namby-pamby

argument. "He's alright. Any man who's not dead after three days' sickness is not sick at all."

Rowand ruled the roost in western Canada for nearly forty years before he finally decided to pack it in and retire to Montreal. He was sixty-five years old; his common-law native wife had died; he had unmarried daughters that he wanted to marry off: it was time to move on. On a May morning in 1854, he stepped into one of his boats, hollered at his men to get moving, and set out for Fort Pitt, the first stop on the long journey east. His son John was in charge of the post at Fort Pitt, and they got to talking that first night. Rowand was never fond of talking, preferring to give orders, but for some reason he told his son that night that, when the time came, he would like to be buried with his kin in Montreal.

The time came the next morning. Two boatmen got into a fight, and John Rowand instinctively moved in to break it up. As he raised his arm to push the two men apart, he dropped dead. John Jr., who may have had something of the old man in him, disregarded his father's last wishes and had him buried promptly at Fort Pitt. But when the word got back to George Simpson that Rowand had asked to be buried in Montreal, Simpson was determined to fulfill his friend's last wish. However, it wasn't that simple in those days to disinter a body and take it half-way across a country for reburial.

Simpson decided to have the body dug up and rendered down to the bones by boiling. There is no record of the exact details of this process — thank goodness for small mercies. Emily Murphy said in her account that the natives who did the job ate a piece of the factor's heart to "inherit his spirit," but that detail isn't mentioned in any other account. In fact, the natives didn't like Rowand. It seems unlikely they would want to inherit any part of him. However, the fact remains that the deed was done, and the bones were packed into a box for shipping. Simpson travelled with them for the first part of the journey by boat to the Red River settlement, but he soon realized his cargo might never make it to Montreal.

"I was afraid they might from a superstitious feeling drop it over board at some time," Simpson wrote in his journal, "and therefore I had it repacked and sent to York Factory for transmission to England by ship from whence it will be forwarded to this place (Montreal)." It took four years for John Rowand's remains to make the round trip. At York Factory on Hudson Bay, they waited for a boat to England. Once in England, they waited for a boat to take them back to Montreal. In Montreal, they waited for George Simpson to pick them up and give them the burial they had been promised.

Simpson was as good as his promise: Rowand's remains are buried beneath a grand memorial in Montreal's Mount Royal Cemetery. But Louise Umfrieville, Rowand's wife, didn't even rate a mention on the marker. She was left behind on the river flats in Edmonton in an old graveyard which gradually disappeared under traffic circles around the Walterdale Bridge.

The unmarried daughters fared much better than their mother, by the way. They married well and got their names on respectable gravestones. Rowand would have been pleased.

~

Father Albert Lacombe had his hand and his heart in just about everything that happened in western Canada for over sixty years, but you would never know it from the no-nonsense words over his last resting place in a crypt at the Roman Catholic Church in St. Albert: **"Pere Lacombe OMI, Born in Quebec in 1827, Came to the west in 1849, Died in 1916, RIP."**

Actually, that should read last resting *places*. Father Lacombe divided himself up at death, which means he gets my nod for most unusual burial arrangements in Alberta. When he died in Calgary in 1916, he asked that his body go back to St. Albert, where he started his missionary work in the West, but that his heart remain in Blackfoot country. I took that to mean that his heart would have returned — dust to dust, etc. — long ago to some sun-parched prairie hill in southern Alberta. How very appropriate, I thought. But no, I learned that his heart remained in a sealed container in a locked closet in a nuns' residence in Calgary for the next seventy-six years. It wasn't buried until 1992. Even then, it wasn't laid to rest on some sacred hillside in Blackfoot country but in the special graveyard behind the Father Lacombe Nursing Home in Calgary.

The Sisters of Charity of Providence looked after it all those years, keeping guard over it at the Lacombe Home, the big red building on the hill in Midnapore, south of Calgary. A home for orphaned children and for old folks who had nowhere to go, the Lacombe Home was just one of the Father's many projects. It changed hands and functions in the 1970s, and the heart went with the Sisters to a nearby nursing home, which is where I saw it. Sister Helen was in charge of it then, a sweet nun who made sure that I understood the significance of the object in her care. This was a sacred object; it was Roman Catholic history; it was western Canadian history. I was not to make jokes about pickles and stuff. She didn't say as much, but I could see she was nervous that I might make light of this important trust.

I had no intention of joking about the heart, but I realized as I listened to Sister Helen, that the revered heart of this wonderful man must be causing problems for the Sisters. Instead of being blessed by the possession of this sacred body part, they were cursed by it, always having to explain it, defend it, and keep it safe. What a coup it would have been for some burglar to steal the heart of Father Lacombe! The responsibility obviously lay heavy on the heart of Sister Helen and her order.

Once she had impressed upon me the solemnity of the moment, she unlocked a corner closet that contained various items used by Father Lacombe — his clock, his razor, his sock darner. (Did Father Lacombe have to darn his own socks? I wanted to ask, but I sensed that Sister Helen would be made nervous by even that much levity.) She showed me photographs of Father Lacombe at his desk and with his great friend and supporter, William Van Horne, the general manager of the CPR. Then and only then did she draw aside the white satin cloth that had been sheltering the famous heart.

At first I was a bit shocked that it looked so much like a heart. While other churches soften reality by hiding human hearts behind red glass or putting them behind candles and gilt trim — Brother Andre's heart in St. Joseph's Oratory Catholic Church in Montreal, for instance, is displayed behind an iron grille door in a stained glass container — this was just a heart preserved in a clear liquid in a clear plastic container.

Sister Helen continued her explanations. "It's been hard to find the right container," she said, "and if there's ever a leak or a need to change the liquid, it requires a trip to a laboratory in Calgary and many anxious moments." She looked so worried, this servant of God and of her church, that it was hard not to wonder if this is what Father Lacombe intended. He took very little heed of his health during his lifetime; it seemed a bit of a contradiction to pay so much attention now. Maybe that was part of the decision to bury the heart once and for all, that and the fact that the world has changed.

From the time Father Lacombe came to western Canada in 1852 until his death in 1916, he was everywhere — spreading the word of God; establishing schools and social services for the needy; mediating disputes between the Indians, the railway and the settlers; ministering to the sick and dying; raising money for good causes. Madline Stover, who in 1991 wrote to me from a senior citizen's lodge in Brooks, remembered the Holy Father coming to her town in eastern Alberta when she was three years old. "Of course," she told me, "there was no Brooks or Alberta at that time, 1903." Her aunt Rose Marie helped set up two saw horses with boards on them and a tablecloth, and that was what Father Lacombe used to perform a Catholic mass for the believers in that area. She would never forget it, she said. And she remembered very well the news of his death in 1916. He was eighty-nine years old.

There was a funeral filled with pomp and circumstance and stirring words, after which the old trooper was carried down to the train station in Calgary for his last trip across the prairies. The CPR had provided a special coach to carry the casket north to Edmonton and then to St. Albert. All along the way beside the tracks, people waited and watched. Some waved when he went by, men took off their hats, women made the sign of the cross, children stood silent.

The Man of the Good Heart — so named by the Blackfoot — had died.

∾

The thought of dividing up human body parts is an unsettling one to most of us, no matter what the circumstances or the reasons, which is why David Kootook emerged as the hero of this story.

It started back on a cold December day in Canada's North. The nurse in charge of the Cambridge Bay nursing station had two critically ill Inuit patients: a twenty-five-year-old pregnant woman who was experiencing some labour complications and fourteen-year-old David Kootook, who was showing symptoms of acute appendicitis. They both required hospitalization in Yellowknife, the charge nurse decided, and she asked

Marten Hartwell to fly them there. Nurse Judy Hill would accompany them on the four-hour flight.

Hartwell had just flown in from Yellowknife and was not at all keen to head out into the cloud and cold again, but risks sometimes have to be taken when medical emergencies arise. So he refuelled, settled his three passengers, and headed south toward Yellowknife. Somewhere, somehow, he got off course and crashed. Judy Hill was killed immediately, the Inuit woman lived a few days, Hartwell's legs seemed to be broken, and David was alright, his appendicitis symptoms gone. It thus fell to David to be the strong one, the legs for Hartwell. It was David who found sleeping bags and food supplies in the wreckage. It was David who arranged makeshift shelter. It was going to be David who walked away from the crash site to find help. This is what he wrote in a letter to his parents in the first week: "The airplane fell....In a few more days, the pilot wants me to walk to Yellowknife. So I must try and walk. I pray to God that I will see you again."

David never did strike out on his own. He died twenty-three days after the crash.

One month after the crash, search planes finally spotted the needle in the northern haystack, and rescuers flew in immediately. They found Marten Hartwell alive and in fairly good shape, considering the ordeal he had just been through. They didn't get the whole picture at first, but when Hartwell greeted them with the words, "Welcome to the Camp of the Cannibal," they began to understand how Hartwell had survived: he had resorted to cannibalism. Had David agreed to go Hartwell's route, he might still be alive, but he had refused.

At first, the rescue was hailed as good news, tinged as it was with sympathy for those who didn't make it. But as the gory details of Hartwell's survival began to leak out, the tenor of the coverage changed. His was not a simple black and white tale of survival in the face of great odds. It was a story that touched upon grey areas that people don't even want to think about.

David Kootook never did make it back to the North. He was buried in the Edmonton Beechmount Cemetery, not marked at all until four years later when David Ward, an Edmonton lawyer and alderman of Inuit background, finally pestered the City of Edmonton into providing the simple flush marker that lies above his grave now. The marker doesn't tell the story at all; it just lists David Kootook's name in English and Inuit with the dates of his short life: August 13, 1958 - December 1972. Once the full story came out, David was nominated for the Governor General's Award for Bravery, and although he seemed in every way to deserve the honour, he didn't get it. David Ward went to bat for him again and again over the award, but the government continued to say that David Kootook's show of courage was not exactly the kind of courage they meant. So David didn't get a medal, but he certainly emerged as the good guy in Peter Tadman's 1991 book *The Survivor*. Maybe a book in one's memory is as good as a posthumous medal.

~

When you drive over the Kicking Horse River in the Kicking Horse Pass in the mountains west of Banff, give a thought to Sir James Hector. He was nearly buried alive there, and because he wasn't, the river and the area got its name.

James Hector was the geologist on the Palliser Expedition sponsored by the British government in 1857-58 to study western Canada. He spent most of his time in the mountains and at one point had to cross a river that did not appeal to his horse. Hector got off to help the horse across, and the horse in turn thanked him for his thoughtfulness by kicking him forcefully in the chest. Hector was unconscious for so long that his companions were convinced he was dead and began to dig a grave. This is how he recalled the incident according to a story in the *Calgary Herald* in the 1920s:

> The pony refused the wild stream and I gave him quite a good blow on the rump. That was the last I knew until I woke in time to behold a grave yawning for me. My friends had decided I was dead and they were doing the respectful act — putting me under the sod. This I sternly refused and having recovered my wind was ready to go off again up that wild stream.

He named the wild stream the Kicking Horse — what else — and, needless to say, never forgot it. On a return visit to Canada in 1903, he planned a trip into the back country to see if he could pinpoint the spot. Unfortunately, just before he was to make his sentimental journey, his son Douglas, who was accompanying him, was stricken with appendicitis. He died

95

in the Revelstoke hospital, and Sir Hector went back to New Zealand, never to return.

Douglas is buried in the Revelstoke Cemetery in an above-ground crypt, the only one of its kind that I've found.

~

I don't know if this story is true, but Annie L. Gaetz told it in the *Red Deer Advocate* in 1971, and she should know. She came to the Red Deer area at the turn of the century, and what she might have missed, she could have learned from her father-in-law, the Rev. Leonard Gaetz, who was one of Red Deer's very first settlers. In fact, Red Deer ended up with so many Gaetz in their midst that jokes were made about having so many Gaetz but hardly any fences!

According to Annie's story, a Mr. Upton died and Mrs. Upton got a wooden coffin from the local undertaker and buried her husband in a corner of their farmland. As soon as this was accomplished, Mrs. Upton harnessed up the team and headed for the United States to apply for the pension she had coming to her as the widow of an American Army veteran. But she was soon back. American authorities told her that her husband had to be buried in the U.S. in a proper soldier's cemetery. Then, and only then, could she apply for the pension.

This was one woman who was not going to miss out on a possible source of income. She ordered a new casket — metal this time — and while she was waiting for it to arrive from Winnipeg, she sold the farm, most of the equipment, and most of the stock. She was all ready to head south as soon as the proper arrangements could be made. But if it wasn't one thing, it was another. When the metal casket finally arrived, it was six inches too short and the wooden casket wouldn't fit inside. There was no way she was going to wait any longer; so she sawed six inches off the end of the wooden casket, in the process of which she sawed her husband's feet off at the ankles. Sometimes these things can't be helped, you understand. Then she put everything back into the coffin and nailed it shut again. This time it fit, but the casket was now too long for the wagon. No matter. She hauled the seat out of the wagon, pushed the casket forward, and used it to sit on. No one ever heard from her again, but I don't doubt for a minute that she got the pension and managed very nicely.

~

The story of the abbreviated Mr. Upton raises the touchy issue of bones. In any construction project, there is always a chance some may turn up, and that's exactly what happened in the late 1970s, when workers began excavating for the light rail transit line that goes from downtown Calgary to the south. As the machines dug into the hill alongside the Chinese cemetery on Macleod Trail, one set of bones showed up. Planners checked their information. There were no grave sites recorded in the area under construction, but just to be sure, they had the workers dig by hand for the next while. In the end, thirty-nine more bodies were unearthed, a total of forty unidentified people.

This wasn't supposed to happen. Planners knew the Chinese grave-yard was awfully close to one section of the new line, but they had made allowance, they thought, and left lots of space. According to all available records, there should not have been any bodies there, but apparently the Chinese community had buried people outside the official cemetery boundaries. Nobody knew just who these forty people were: neither the city, who had been keeping the official records since 1938, nor the Chinese community itself. So without too much fanfare or media attention — how did they manage that? — the bones were reburied in a group grave. A Chinese clergyman said a few ecumenical words at the time of burial, ecumenical because he had no idea who he was speaking about and what their faith might have been. This grave was not marked either, but at least it's on city records now.

There have been other old bones unearthed in the West as roads were built, buildings went up, farmers plowed their fields. It was an un-pleasant experience generally, but it wasn't taken too seriously until just a few years ago. Suddenly the western world discovered a social con-science. No longer was it possible to dismiss some old bones as "just an Indian," or "just an old geezer who won't mind being disturbed." Michael Dawe at the Red Deer Museum and Archives, for one, is very glad that this turnabout has taken place. There used to be an old cemetery near the tracks in downtown Red Deer, and because nobody really cared, the graves just gradually disappeared under roads and the buildings of a nearby brewery. Had it contained anyone of "importance," anyone other than natives and the odd child or two, he thinks it might have been cared for with greater diligence. As it was, he came along too late to make a difference, at least for that particular graveyard.

The other factor that has forced a reexamination of the way we treat the old bones in our midst is the media. Old bones, they have discovered, make good copy. We've gone from one extreme to another — from treating unexpected graves and unidentified remains as a bit of a nuisance, an unpleasant discovery, to treating them all like the latest episode of a soap opera. Somewhere, there has to be a caring and dignified middle ground.

~

THE LAST WORD: Epitaphs in the 1800s in other parts of Canada often referred matter-of-factly to "mouldering in the dust" or "the once loved form now cold and dead" or "death's cold arms." But Alberta has very few of these doleful last words because we're just too new. Our history in graveyards didn't begin until the early 1900s, by which time the fashion in epitaphs had changed. Mostly, we used Christian sentiments like the ones in the picture below of the Myer graves.

Ever Remembered, Ever Loved

~

Vermilion Cemetery

Stories of Catastrophe

When you come my grave to see
Prepare yourself to follow me
Prepare in time, Make no delay
For I was quickly called away.

...from the grave of James Fairfield
(died February 2, 1928, aged 54 years)
in the Edson Cemetery

Like James Fairfield, many Albertans were quickly called away, taken by catastrophic events such as mines that blew up, ships that went down, diseases that could not be controlled. Life was one big poker game in the early days — you won some, you lost some, and to live to a ripe old age was a major accomplishment. Amazingly, the province's graveyards do not mention the three catastrophes that took more lives in Alberta's history than anything other than world wars. You would never know that thousands of us died from smallpox, influenza, or tuberculosis. It's a puzzling omission.

To be fair, the smallpox epidemic happened in the 1870s, long before formal graveyards were established. It killed one-third to one-half the population of western Canada at the time, a terrible scourge. Victims were buried or left where they died. But by the time the influenza epidemic came along in 1918-19, there were established graveyards. You would expect to find the word "flu" here and there, but you don't. Nor do you see the word "tuberculosis" on gravemarkers in the North, where the disease swept whole communities. These were all catastrophes of enormous scale, but our graveyards don't tell the story at all. Maybe they were so dreaded that they were too awful even for the graveyard.

But the non-disease catastrophes — the accidents and natural disasters, the drownings and fires — do show up in our graveyards. They're not nearly as quiet. Some, in fact, have been turned into historical sites.

Take, for example, the Hillcrest Cemetery, a hauntingly beautiful spot along the Crowsnest Pass highway east of Frank that speaks volumes about life and death in mining communities in the early days.

The people who decided to make mass graves after the Hillcrest Mine disaster did so because of numbers and haste and expediency, I'm sure, but they couldn't have found a more gripping way to tell the awful story. The first things you see in the Hillcrest Cemetery are little white picket fences that go on and on, eventually joining to enclose large empty spaces. Well, mostly empty. There's an occasional gravemarker, leaning one way or another, but mostly it's empty space within those wandering walls.

There are four such enclosures marking the areas where the victims were buried after the worst mining accident in Canadian history on June 19, 1914. A total of 189 men died on that terrible morning, and most of them are buried at Hillcrest. Very few are marked individually in the graveyard; their names are not there. But the story speaks for itself within those empty fences: the story of men who routinely went underground to mine for coal, the story of men who sometimes lost the gamble underground, the story of families who couldn't afford a gravemarker for their loved one, the story of lives blown to bits in more ways than one. One of the few gravemarkers within a fence is there in memory of Wasil Elick, aged forty-eight years. The day after he was killed in the Hillcrest Mine, his wife had a baby.

It was unthinkably awful, all of it. The Hillcrest Mine was considered one of the best. The labyrinth of tunnels and shafts and runways was regularly inspected for build-up of gases and coal dust, but in spite of the precautions, something went terribly wrong that morning. Without warning, it blew up. Something had ignited the methane gas that was always present in greater or lesser quantities in nooks and crannies of the mine. The fire spread through the tunnels until it hit a pocket of coal dust, then it blew. Even buildings outside the mine opening were flattened and burned. It couldn't have been worse. If the miners inside weren't killed instantly by falling rocks or by the force of the explosion, they faced black damp, the air that is left after the oxygen has been burned off. Black damp is mostly carbon monoxide, and it kills as surely as fire and explosion.

The families gathered at the mine entrance, watching and waiting. Every time another survivor or body was brought up, they would surge forward to see who it was, then go back to watching and waiting. Police from nearby detachments took on the grisly job of identifying burned and broken bodies. They never did get it quite right. Some of the bodies were so broken that it was hard to match the pieces, and in the end, the police had an extra leg. Rather than distress the families any further, they just put the extra limb in with someone else. Somewhere in that mass grave is a coffin with three legs.

Funerals began the following Sunday and went on all day. First the Catholics had a service, then the Anglicans. Together they formed a cortege and moved toward the graveyard. Other Protestant services were held in the afternoon, followed by more burials. The graves had all been dug in advance — one foot apart in long wandering lines. That first day, 150 men were buried. The remaining bodies went to graveyards elsewhere in the Crowsnest Pass. Some went home to Nova Scotia.

How men could go into that mine again is hard to understand, but the mine reopened within a few months and continued to operate until the 1940s. When it was finally closed, the troubled tunnels were sealed, the equipment sold and moved away, the tipple torn down. Nothing was left except white picket fences that both hold and tell the story of the Hillcrest Mine Disaster.

~

The little graves at the old Victoria Mission are another sad sight, so alone and silent. It was the silence I noticed first. Blackbirds or magpies ordinarily own a graveyard, and they're not particularly keen on having company, wheeling and squawking about until they're sure you mean them no harm. But the McDougall graves had no one standing guard or flying past. They were utterly alone, prisoners of their chain link fence. Even the nearby river proceeded silently between its banks, as if there were a sign somewhere down there saying Caution: Children at Rest Here.

They are not easy to find. Alberta history books toss off the line that the McDougall graves are at Pakan, as if Pakan still existed, or they say the graves are at the Victoria Mission. Both statements are true. It's just that neither name can be found on an Alberta map anymore. You have to get on highway 855 between Andrew and Smoky Lake and watch for the directional signs. Now a historic site, the graves are located on the north side of the North Saskatchewan River, east of the highway.

There are more signs when you get to the site, interpretive signs that explain the scattered buildings and tell just who did what at this isolated mission. Like all historical projects, the signs are interesting and worthwhile, but they can't beat the little graves for telling the story of a man who had a mission and in the process left three lives behind.

Rev. George McDougall came to western Canada in 1862 to establish the Methodist church among the Indians. He believed, as did all Christians in those days, that it was the responsibility of civilized Christians to bring both their religion and their civilization to those who had neither. Such a goal seems arrogant by today's standards, but McDougall was not at all arrogant. He was a humble servant of the Lord — that's how he would have expressed it. His first major mission in Alberta, the Victoria Mission, was established on the North Saskatchewan River about seventy miles north and east of Edmonton. The idea was that the mission would be an integrated operation with a church on site, as well as a grinding mill, a model farm, and a school for the native children. McDougall would teach the Christian faith by good works as well as good words. At least, that was the theory.

The only trouble was that the mission didn't have a hospital or a doctor; more to the point, it didn't have the smallpox vaccine. In 1870, a terrible smallpox epidemic swept across western Canada. The Indians and Metis were particularly susceptible, but the scattered white folk got it too, including the McDougall family. Eleven-year-old Flora was the first to die in her household. She "entered into rest" on October 13, 1870.

Ere sin could blight or sorrow fade
Death came with friendly care
The opening bud to Heaven conveyed
And bade it blossom there.

Her older sister Georgiana followed two weeks later on November 1, 1870, aged nineteen years. Her marker says:

I shall be satisfied when
I awake with thy likeness.

A year later, Abigail Steinhauer, the first wife of McDougall's son John, died at age twenty-three years, ten months, also of smallpox. She is buried with Flora and Georgiana on the banks of the North Saskatchewan. Mrs. McDougall Sr. was the only family member who didn't get the dread disease. She worked night and day to minister to her own family and to the Indians in the area, but her nursing skills added to her devout Christian belief were no match for smallpox. It was not to be denied.

The same thing was happening all over western Canada. McDougall's Catholic competition, Father Albert Lacombe in St. Albert, could only console and bury. He had no cure either, and he certainly hadn't intended that one of his first lessons in Christianity for the Indians would be the ceremony of Christian burial, but that's what happened. So many were buried in the St. Albert Cemetery next to Father Lacombe's mission that in later years the area had to be closed to further burials. They kept finding bodies in the graveyard that they had no record of. Indians did not mark their dead with marble headstones the way the McDougalls had, which is why the McDougall graves are just about the only sign of the terrible smallpox epidemic of 1870. No wonder they seem so lonely. Not only are they alone, but they alone can tell the awful story of the smallpox epidemic of 1870.

The loss of the McDougall daughters to smallpox was not the family's only tragedy. In the years that followed, the McDougalls moved from the Victoria Mission to Edmonton and then to Morley, each time establishing a church and a mission among the Indians of the area. While the family was at Morley, Rev. McDougall went on a routine buffalo hunting expedition and never returned. It was a cold January day in 1876, the hunt had been successful, and McDougall had volunteered to ride ahead to the base camp. He never arrived. Two weeks of searching later, his body was finally found. Mrs. McDougall described it this way in a letter to her mother:

> He was found lying as if some kind hand had been there; one
> hand lay on his breast, the other a little on the side, his eyes and
> lips closed, and a smile on his countenance, his legs and feet in
> the right position ready for burial. When he lay down to die he
> must have had great presence of mind.

He was buried on a hill within sight of the church he had built at Morley. His gravemarker says:

Sacred to the Memory of
Rev. George McDougall
Aged 54 years

The deceased was for 16 years chairman of the Wesleyan missions in the northwest. He lost his way on the prairie about 40 miles east of this place on January 24, 1876. His body was found on the 5th of the following month and interred here by his sorrowing family who have erected this tribute in his memory.

The same words appear on a more elaborate marker beside the church, but the best place to read them is in the graveyard itself where George McDougall lies, no more and no less than the Indians he came to serve in the first place. His wife, as ever, is by his side.

⌒

There's an empty space in the Calgary Union graveyard — quite a large space considering that this graveyard is pretty well full to the brim. But at this one spot, there are only trees, grass, and the occasional dandelion that gets away from its keepers.

This is where the victims of the 1918 flu epidemic were buried in haste, in fear, and in confusion. Records weren't kept, bodies were buried quickly to stop the spread of the disease, grave locations weren't marked. It was an awful time; death was everywhere. The details that would normally have been taken care of, the ceremony that would normally have accompanied a burial — none of it happened. Not in the heat of the epidemic, at least. Later on, when families and graveyard officials tried to figure out who was buried where, they couldn't. The area had to be closed to further burials and left as is.

In Grande Prairie, flu victims were buried near Bear Creek in an area chosen because the soil was sandy and easily dug up. There wasn't time to dig through the hard clay in the other graveyard, or to thaw frozen ground. So this sandy hill was chosen, and day after day, sorrowing families came to leave a loved one on the hillside near the creek. Sometimes they marked the grave, and sometimes they didn't. It depended. If the rest of the family was well, they might find time to put up a wooden cross. But if others in the family were ill, the job was never done.

The wooden crosses rotted away over the years, and there were fears of vandalism, so in 1975, the city set the area aside as a historical site and erected a cairn. It's the only place I have been able to find the word "flu" written in a graveyard. Yet if the word is mentioned in the company of anyone who has a long memory, it always brings the same results. Sad tales of sudden and senseless death. Shaking of the head. Memories of a fight with an enemy that wouldn't stand up and be counted. The flu was a cruel and capricious enemy that killed up to 50,000 Canadians in the years of 1918 and 1919.

The virus came to Canada with the soldiers returning from World War I, some of whom lived through the horrors of war overseas only to be felled by the flu at home. Doctors now say that most of those deaths were actually the result of pneumonia that followed the general weakening of the system caused by the virulent flu strain. But you couldn't tell that to the people who were battling the awful disease in 1918 and 1919. It was the flu they were battling and the flu that was killing them. As for what caused it, they weren't sure. The telephone operator in Gadsby was observed looking out of a window with her forehead pressed against the frosty glass. A week later, she was dead of the flu, and people wondered if the frosty window might have had something to do with the death.

Lacking information and facilities, communities just did the best they could. Hotels and schools were turned into hospitals. In Bindloss, the poolroom became the hospital, the pool tables hospital beds. Doctors were few and far between, or far too busy, so Volunteer Aid Detachment (VAD) workers were recruited from around the province. Sometimes the VAD workers had some nursing or first aid training. Sometimes they didn't. Gertrude Charteris was a VAD sent to Drumheller at the height of the epidemic there. The conductor wouldn't let her off the train until she showed all her papers. Drumheller was off limits. The whole place was quarantined.

Folk remedies abounded. An old-timer in the Verdant Valley area heard that sulphur prevented the disease. Somebody told him to sprinkle a spoonful on hot coals and let the fumes permeate the house. On the theory that if a little worked, then a whole lot should work even better, he put about a cupful of sulphur on a fire smouldering in the wood stove and caused such a stink that the household had to spend the night in the barn. As it turned out, they escaped the flu but were never able to say for sure whether it had been the sulphur, the fresh air in the barn, or none of the above.

When George Webber from the Carbon area loaded up the back seat of his 490 Chevrolet with food for the neighbourhood bachelors who had no one to look after them, he wore a mask infused with eucalyptus oil. He would make the mask out of cheesecloth, then sprinkle the aromatic oil upon it before covering his nose and mouth. He, too, survived.

Most people wore masks. That was the first thing that Milton Switzer in Drumheller noticed upon his recovery — masks everywhere. "They reminded me of pictures I had seen of Turkish harem women," he wrote. "Only their eyes showed above these sheets of white gauze they wore over the lower part of their faces."

Dr. Judson Snyder of the Ghost Pine area didn't think masks made much sense. His family was constantly exposed anyway, he thought, so he didn't force the children to wear the masks, and he often left his own at home. But the local policeman would have nothing to do with that foolishness. He told the doctor he would fine him if he didn't wear his mask as prescribed. Dr. Snyder lived through the epidemic.

And when the battle was lost, as it so often was, the community continued to do its best. In Olds, for example, straw was put down on the streets so that the clip-clopping of the horses enroute to the graveyard would not frighten and dishearten others who were sick.

It was an absolutely incredible part of our western history, which makes it all the more incredible that I can't find a word about it in our graveyards.

~

Tuberculosis is another catastrophe that's silent in our graveyards. It devastated entire native communities in the North, but there's no mention of it in northern graveyards. You can often guess at its presence, however. In a more or less abandoned cemetery next to the old St. Joseph's Roman Catholic Church near Fort Vermilion are row upon row of little white crosses with the same last name on them. Seeing them, reading the name over and over again, suddenly makes the tragedy human instead of statistical.

Dr. Mary Percy Jackson of Keg River certainly did what she could to prevent those tragedies, but in the 1930s in the North, the only options were bed rest, which Dr. Jackson could do something about, and isolation, which she could not. It was not the Indian way to leave a sick person alone; in fact, quite the opposite. When there was illness or death, families and friends gathered. In most cases, Dr. Jackson now says, that made good sense. But tuberculosis is spread by sneezing and by contact with food and drinking water, so the sociable habits of the natives meant that the disease spread far and wide and quickly.

She wrote repeatedly to the federal government requesting the tuberculosis vaccine that had been used in some other parts of Canada. The government was no help. As a matter of fact, they kept statistics about Indian deaths by tuberculosis separate from Canadian statistics so that Canada wouldn't look so bad. And then, according to Dr. Jackson, who doesn't hesitate to call a spade a spade, they just never mentioned the Indian stats. In 1946, for example, the tuberculosis rate among Indian people in Alberta was 875 per 100,000 compared to 47 per 100,000 for Canadians generally. No wonder the government didn't mention the numbers.

The provincial government finally got in the act and set up some beds for tuberculosis patients in the Baker Sanatorium in Calgary and the Charles Camsell Sanatorium in Edmonton. Things slowly got better. Treatment improved, transportation got easier, prevention was taken seriously. But there is a cairn in the St. Albert municipal graveyard that demonstrates we hadn't quite finished the job as far as caring for the victims of tuberculosis is concerned.

The cairn lists the names of some ninety-eight people who died of tuberculosis in the Charles Camsell Hospital in Edmonton. They were originally buried in the area around the cairn, land that was part of an Indian residential school at the time, and they were marked only by wooden crosses that eventually rotted, fell over, and burned. By the 1980s, there was nothing left to tell the story. And so it would have remained, had it not been for Elva Taylor, who was head nurse at the Camsell from 1946 to1966. She couldn't bear the thought of so many of her patients remaining unmarked, unknown, so she raised money for a monument, pricked the conscience of the government, and researched the names of those who lay somewhere in the grass. In 1990, the stone cairn was unveiled to commemorate **"the resting places of those who have been called to the home of the great spirit."**

~

Just as epidemics and industrial accidents like the one at Hillcrest claimed lives without warning, our lakes and rivers could also turn upon us and wreak havoc. Water was a mixed blessing for western pioneers. Rain meant good crops, but it also meant high water in the creeks and rivers that had to be forded. Bridges were few and far between. There were a lot of drowning accidents.

Thus, there are gravemarkers like the one at Whitecourt for the Prestlien family, father, mother, and four children who drowned when crossing the Athabasca River. They had crossed the river safely many times before in their team and wagon, but this time the river was so high that the wagon somehow got hung up on a barbed wire fence hidden under the raging waters. The harness broke, the wagon tipped, and the family was swept away.

The actual details of a drowning incident are not usually included on the gravemarker. Sometimes the facts are brutally brief, as they are on the marker for Charles Blake in the Camrose Cemetery, which says simply: "**Born 1915, Drowned 1929.**"

The Robertson grave in the Calgary Union Cemetery tells both a unique story and an all too familiar one. Mrs. Susan Robertson was buried at sea, the marker says, while she was returning from China. I haven't been able to find out what happened on that fateful voyage, but I do know that she was returning from a visit to her son Thompson, who worked as an engineer in China. On the other side of the marker is the information that her husband, the Rev. Angus Robertson, first Presbyterian minister in Calgary, died in Medicine Hat in 1890. Ironically, water was more than likely his undoing as well. He started his ministry in Calgary, establishing what is now the Knox United Church, but he had moved on to bring the Christian message to railway construction camps in the mountains. In one of those camps, he contracted typhoid fever, a disease that is carried in water and food. The camps were notorious for their carelessness in placing toilet facilities too close to water sources. Although Rev. Robertson was treated at the Medicine Hat hospital, the disease had its way.

~

When I found the Bartschi gravestone in the Stettler Cemetery, I stumbled onto another story of cruel waters. The Bartschi stone told the tale of two brothers: Theo who lived a long life and Christian who perished May 29, 1914, on the Empress of Ireland. That was the first mention I found of the Empress of Ireland, but there are two more in the Calgary Union Cemetery.

My first thought was that the incident might have been war-related, but the Empress of Ireland was a Canadian Pacific ship enroute from Quebec City to Liverpool, England. Less than twelve hours into the voyage, when the ship was still in the St. Lawrence River, it was rammed by a Norwegian collier and damaged so severely that it sank within ten minutes. Most passengers never knew what hit them — it was the middle of the night in the middle of a terrible fog. There were enough lifeboats on board, if there had been time for any kind of orderly evacuation, but there was no time. The 452 who managed to survive did so because some of the lifeboats broke loose from the ship when it went down. The rest of the passengers and crew perished — 1,027 went down with the ship.

Calgary's *Daily Herald* reported in black headlines: "Over 20 Calgarians Perish on Empress" and followed with pages of details about the accident and the victims. In a corner of the frenzied reporting was this little tale under a much smaller headline, "Calgary Man Looks for His Loved Ones."

> Haunting newspaper offices here, hoping against hope that some further survivors of the ill-fated Empress may be heard of, is George Howarth of Calgary whose wife and two children are among the lost. Howarth is a stolid Englishman usually, but the realization of his dreadful bereavement, following hours of suspense, has so benumbed him that he can scarcely tell his own name. He saw his loved ones on the boat on Thursday evening and was returning to Calgary when the news of the grim tragedy reached him and he got off the train at Toronto to await details. He will probably go to Quebec City to see if any of the bodies recovered are of his wife and children.

I don't know if the bodies of Howarth's family members were ever recovered, but there is a marker in the Calgary Union Cemetery in memory of Beatrice and her two children, Emmie and Leonard.

The other marker I found was in memory of Wm. and Mary Garnett, who were part of a Canadian Salvation Army contingent headed to England for an International Salvation Army Congress. Of the 190 Salvationists who set out on the journey, only twenty survived. All these years later, the Salvation Army still holds a memorial service every year in Toronto's Mount Pleasant Cemetery and remembers in an impressive monument that awful morning on the St. Lawrence.

~

THE LAST WORD: On a small sweet gravemarker in the Fort Macleod Cemetery are the words: Thomas Saul, born Oct.11, 1882, drowned July 24, 1884.

Asleep in Jesus, blessed sleep,
From which none ever wake to weep.

~

Cluny Cemetery

Stories of War

Rest, soldier, rest, thy warfare's o'er,
Sleep the sleep that knows no breaking
Dream of battlefields no more
Days of danger, nights of waking.

...An excerpt of Sir Walter Scott's "The Lady of the
Lake" on the grave of Augustus E. Moore
in the Tees Cemetery

What battlefields? I asked myself as I stood before the grey granite marker that belongs to Augustus Moore. According to the biographical information, he died in 1914 at the age of seventy-four, which means he would have been too old to have fought in the Boer War in South Africa (1899-1902) or the Spanish American War of 1898. He was born in Sullivan County in New York, so it's unlikely that he fought on foreign shores, although he could have slipped up to Canada for the North West Rebellion. Was that his battlefield? Is that how he came to be in Canada? The only other war that might explain the epitaph was the American Civil War (1861-65). Was he once upon a time a Union soldier under the command of General Ulysses S. Grant? Was he among those fighting to keep the American Union intact, fighting to end slavery in the United States of America?

Mind you, he may not have been an official soldier at all. Maybe his battles to make a living in central Alberta at the beginning of the century were so strenuous that he felt like a soldier. Or maybe his family saw him as a faithful old fighter who deserved fighting words on his tombstone.

Whatever the reasons, the words seemed just right. My father was an old soldier too, not literally but figuratively, as he did battle over the years with his crops, the weather, and the cows that never seemed to come home. After yet another early frost, he would look at the drooping garden behind our house, blackened produce that signalled even worse damage in the fields beyond, and he would say, "Next year, it will be better. Wait until next year." We couldn't understand his patience, his endurance. How could he stand there, year after year, and let nature kick him around? How could he let himself be beaten?

In fact, he was not beaten. It takes more than battles to be beaten. Old farmers know that. So do old soldiers.

~

The North West Rebellion was the most Canadian of all wars, fought on Canadian soil, both sides under Canadian rule, the battles arising from anger and betrayal felt by the natives and Metis of Canada on the one hand, and on the other a refusal by the government to negotiate and listen. What could be more Canadian? If it happened today, it would be called a constitutional wrangle, because that's essentially what it was. Seeing surveyors from Ottawa come out and stake out what had traditionally been their land, the Indians and Metis of western Canada feared they were losing control. They were being pushed around, pushed off their land and homes without any kind of consultation or permission. They protested without much effect until Louis Riel took up their cause in 1870 and forced the government to make some concessions.

By 1885, however, the concessions could no longer hold back the hunger and despair brought about by the disappearance of the buffalo. Without buffalo, the natives had to depend on Indian agents, on handouts and rules that they had played no part in making. It was a tinder box asking for a light, and the match was struck one spring morning in Frog Lake.

Frog Lake is on the Alberta/Saskatchewan border just south of Cold Lake. There is no town there as such, just a corner store. The land is mostly scrub brush, the road is mostly narrow and dusty, and it's about the last place you'd expect to find an important piece of history. But the graveyard, a rather low key affair, is there to testify to the event. I say "low key" because there are very few signs announcing the location of the Frog Lake graveyard even though it's an historic site, and once you do find it, it's pretty quiet about its reason for existence. Perhaps the whole idea of a massacre of one group of people by another group is too politically sensitive right now to mention; therefore, the Frog Lake site is understated, to say the least.

It's a small corner of land right next to the dirt road that goes east of the Frog Lake store. You see the stone cairn first and then, in its shadow, seven black and white crosses and one RCMP marker. They have obviously been there for awhile. On the edge of the bush on the east side are new wooden pillars with interpretive information on them.

The Historic Sites Board of Canada cairn is no-nonsense in its explanation of events. It states simply:

North West Rebellion.
Frog Lake Massacre.
Here on 2nd April, 1885
Rebel Indians Under
Big Bear Massacred
Rev. Father Leon Adelard Fafard, O.M.I.
Rev. Father Felix Marchand, O.M.I.
Indian Agent Thomas Quinn
Farm Instructor John Delaney
John Alexander Gowanlock
William Campbell Gilchrist
George Dill
Charles Gouin
John Williscroft
They Took Prisoners
Mrs. Theresa Delaney,
Mrs. Theresa Gowanlock.

History being somewhat subject to change, the recently installed interpretive panels give a slightly different slant to the events of that day.

In the early morning, Indians went about collecting all the arms of the white people. After breakfast, the whites were herded into the church, a foreshortened mass was said, then the Indians tried to move everyone to their camp. But Tom Quinn refused to go, the last it seems in a long series of disagreements between he and Wandering Spirit, and the war chief shot him. Whether it was planned to kill the white people, none can say. But when one started shooting, pretty soon everybody was shooting. A few brief moments of fury, dust, and smoke and nine people lay dead or dying on the ground. Theresa Delaney and Theresa Gowanlock escaped death because the Indians disdained to kill women.

What followed was a most confusing time. The battles of what is now called the North West Rebellion were confusing, the participants were often confused about just what was happening, the reports to the outside world ranged from one extreme to another, and white settlers scattered across the prairies didn't know whether to run or stay. In the end, government troops overwhelmed the insurgents and their leader Louis Riel surrendered.

There was never any doubt about the outcome of Riel's trial. No matter how brilliant his defense or how noble his own sentiments or how just his cause, he was to be hanged and be done with. The government was tired of his interference. So he was led to a scaffold in the prison grounds at Regina, November 16, 1885, and that should have been that. The trouble should have disappeared with the troublemaker, but it didn't. Land rights and self-government for the Indians and Metis of Canada are still unresolved.

Riel was buried in St. Boniface, Manitoba, in the cemetery beside the cathedral.

~

The North West Rebellion shows up in a number of Alberta graveyards, not just the one at Frog Lake. In the St. Albert Catholic Cemetery, for instance, are the graves of Father Marchand and Father Fafard, the priests who died at Frog Lake. They were originally buried with the other slain men, but some years later, their bodies were moved to a special section in the St. Albert graveyard.

You can often spot references to the Alberta Field Force of 1885 in other graveyards, a sure give-away that the soldier was part of the military that was quickly organized to contain Riel. In Calgary's Burnsland Cemetery, for example, is a Legion marker for Trooper J. Chas. Gordon who died March 17, 1934. His war record is explained simply as **"N.W. Rebellion 1885."**

Sometimes just one of the battles is mentioned. There is a simple bronze plaque on a grave in the Innisfail Cemetery that says:

In Memory of James Octavius Bennett
Born Sept. 2, 1848, Tideswell, Derbyshire, Eng.
Batoche 1885, 35 York Rangers
Died Nov. 10, 1909

And there are the graves of old soldiers like this one in the Edmonton Cemetery, which among a long list of military connections mentions the Riel or North West Rebellion:

In Memory of Arthur Henry Griesbach
Died at Chemainus, B.C. 21st Nov. 1916
Retired 30th Nov. 1904 after 30 years service
In RNWM Police Rank Superintendent
Previous Service in the 15th Hussars
Cape Mounted Rifles and 1st Ontario Rifles in R.
Rebellion
Colonel in Militia of Canada 5th Nov. 1912

Arthur Henry Griesbach's son, W.A. "Billy" Griesbach, was also a soldier, born too late for the North West Rebellion but just in time for the Boer War in 1899. The story goes that Billy was so anxious to join his father's profession that he tied a piece of coal to his back to reach the necessary enlistment weight of 140 pounds. Once on the battlefield in South Africa, he distinguished himself as a soldier, but he also began a systematic study of war — how to prepare for war, how best to wage war, how to win a war. He made copious notes, read ancient and modern military theorists, and in whatever way possible prepared himself for World War I, which he never doubted would happen. When it did, he was ready. He distinguished himself again, as much for his personal courage as for his leadership.

When he came home safely in 1918, Griesbach went on to become a member of parliament and a senator, but he never stopped studying the subject that fascinated him the most. His grave marked simply **"A Great Soldier"** is located next to his father's, father and son together having been involved in more battles than most Canadians have ever heard of!

~

At the other end of the scale is a gravemarker that's not nearly so grand but still claiming connection to Riel. It's a small, grey, almost-lost-in-the-weeds marker that I found in High Prairie, a northern Alberta town that didn't even exist when the North West Rebellion took place in 1885. It says simply:

In Loving Memory of Peter Tomkins
Born Dec. 10, 1873 Died Jan. 21, 1940
Veteran 1885 Rebellion

I got interested after I did the arithmetic. After all, if Peter Tomkins had been born in 1873, he would have been twelve at the time of the North West Rebellion. Were the dates wrong, or was he perhaps a child captured with his family during the uprising? When I asked a local historian, she couldn't help me, and the local history book didn't mention the Tomkins family either. It seemed to be as big a mystery to the locals as it was to me. Who was this person in northern Alberta who claimed to be a veteran of one of the unhappiest episodes in all of Canadian history?

I checked out Frog Lake first, but there wasn't a Tomkins mentioned in any of the historical accounts. Since he wasn't part of the Alberta side of the battle, then perhaps he was part of the Saskatchewan side. I phoned the archives in Regina, and sure enough, there was a Peter Tompkins — this one with a "p" — in their records. He had been detained and kept prisoner for several weeks while the battles raged on and off around Batoche.

It was the right Peter Tomkins. The birth date on his gravemarker was out by several years and should probably have been 1864 or 1865, which would have made him about twenty years old at the time of the Riel uprising. He got himself into trouble when Riel's men found him up a telegraph pole trying to repair a line that they had destroyed in order to prevent communication with the outside world. They ordered him down and detained him along with about twenty other prisoners in various locations around Batoche. When Riel was captured and charged with treason, Tomkins was one of those who testified at his trial.

After the trial, Tomkins became a farm instructor at the Poundmaker reserve in Saskatchewan. Then he moved on to the Saddle Lake reserve in Alberta, probably to do something similar there. In 1907, he was appointed Dominion Land Agent for the Peace River country, and he stayed in the North from then on. He used to say to his son, another Peter Tomkins:

Pete, some day these scissor bills that they've got who put Riel to hang him, they'll be gone and another outfit will spring up and they'll see the mistake that these guys made. They should never have hanged Riel. He never did anything worse than a good Union man would do to his group and someday they'll build a monument.

~

The most obvious sign in our graveyards of official military service are the Legion monuments, the simple grey markers that fill the Fields of Honour. Row on row, like so many soldiers at attention, the markers all look alike. Name, rank, serial number, name of unit served, date of death, and that's about all. You can find a sweet sentiment here and there, a longing word or two added by the family, but the Legion believes firmly in the principle of equality. A general and a private get the same grave-stone if it is provided by the Last Post fund, which supplies a headstone free to any veteran. If the family wants a grander memorial, then they must buy it themselves and decide upon the wording.

Simple as they may be, the right words make such a difference. I was stopped in my tracks, for example, when I found added to a standard Legion marker the words, **"We shall remember him as he was, a dear son and a good brave lad. Signed by Mother and Dad."** How can your heart not crack? The marker was in memory of Arthur Bloxham, RAFVR, died September 1, 1943, and buried in Calgary's Burnsland Cemetery.

On the marker of Flight Lieutenant Ernest G. Ford, RAF, died December 10, 1942, and buried at Burnsland as well, is another message from grieving parents: **"Ever in our thoughts, From his broken hearted Mother and Dad."**

Lest you get the idea that the Canadian government brought back the bodies of young men and women who died in active service overseas and buried them in their home town, they did not. Young Bloxham and Ford may have been killed in training accidents in the Calgary area, or they may have come home with injuries so serious that they died shortly thereafter. Had they died on the battlefield, they would not have been in the Calgary graveyard. The fighting men and women who died overseas were, as a rule, buried near the site of their death and then later moved to Commonwealth cemeteries in Europe or Asia. Thus, it is not the young soldiers who are at rest in Canadian graveyards, it is the old ones, the men and women who lived through the wars and then came home to die, whether that happened sooner or later. The overseas graveyards contain the ones who didn't make it home.

They are awful and wonderful, those overseas graveyards. The Canadian government and the governments of the various host countries maintain them beautifully, but all the beauty and respect can't hide the numbers — neither the numbers of people who were killed, nor the numbers on the markers, numbers like eighteen and nineteen and twenty-two, the ages of the men who died in the great wars. My own son was twenty-two when I visited several of the Commonwealth graves, and I was a wreck as I looked at the unhappy statistics. How did those mothers let their sons go away to almost certain death? I wouldn't do it, I told myself, but I also knew that it is not fair to apply the sensibilities of the 1990s to a world I didn't understand in either 1914 or 1939.

Had I lived then, I, too, might have added to my son's gravemarker: **"Whatever is, is best."** After all, what else was there to say? Those words are written on the marker of Captain Hatton Harriss, 82 Battn. CEF, who died February 16, 1922, and is buried in Calgary's Union Cemetery.

Or if I had been able to think at all, I hope I would have used words like the ones on the Legion marker of LAC Edward W.R. Bolton, RCAF, died April 6, 1943, and buried at Burnsland in Calgary: "**Here a boy be sweet through all the singing season and departed as he came.**" I know we don't generally talk about our boys being sweet, but they are. We don't use metaphors for their youth like the "singing season," but it is. And one mother — for I hear a mother in those words — said so.

I don't know who speaks in another of my favourite war gravemarkers. It is a small, rounded, white marble marker, almost lost to sight among much grander tombstones in the old part of Union Cemetery in Calgary. It's not in a military section but it says simply:

In Memory of Dear Old Fred
Killed in Action Vimy Ridge
April 9, 1917, Aged 21 Years.

There is no last name, no indication of who erected the memorial. It has to be a memorial only, since Fred's body would not have been returned to Canada. But who would have made this gesture? Who wanted Fred to be remembered in his own land? Not a sweetheart, surely. She wouldn't have called him dear *old* Fred. Not parents. Parents don't talk like that about precious young sons. Friends, maybe? Comrades who also fought in that terrible battle and made it home?

Of the 100,000 Canadians who took part in the terrible battle on Vimy Ridge between April 9 and 14, 1917, a total of 3,598 were killed. Among them, on the very first day of battle, was dear old Fred.

~

For some families, the knowledge of a grave in another country is not enough. They want to see the name of their loved one at home as well, which is why you'll often find the name of a war casualty added to a family marker. Particularly was this true following the First World War.

In the Mount Pleasant Cemetery in Edmonton is a mother who outlived her young son by many years, but she still has his name with hers.

In Loving Memory of
Harriet Dixon
1870-1946
And son Pte. Herbert Dixon
Missing in Action
Oct. 8, 1916 — 17 yrs.
Forever With the Lord

The McLeod family gravemarker in the Edmonton Cemetery names Kenneth McLeod, a pioneer of the Edmonton area of 1881, his wife Anne, and their son Roderick, who was born in 1902 and **"Lost in the sinking of the Patrol Vessel Galiano, October 30, 1918."**

Another Edmonton gravemarker tells a sad story of lives lost overseas. At the bottom of the McQueen marker for Rev. David George McQueen, minister of First Presbyterian Church in Edmonton for many years, and his wife Catherine Robertson McQueen, is information about their son.

L/Cpl Alexander Robertson McQueen, P.P.C.L.I.
Died of Wounds at Ypres, June 4, 1916, aged 23 years
Buried in Lijssenthoek Military cemetery

The old cemetery at Banff contains a number of family plots, among them the Dowler family plot. At the foot of their space is a small plaque that says:

Lieutenant George Dowler E D F C
Royal Air Force
1894-1918
Sleeps in Flanders Fields

The date of his death isn't included on the memorial plaque, perhaps because it hurt too much. He was killed November 10, 1918, one day before Armistice was declared and the war was over. His sister Marjorie wrote to me about her warrior brother and told more of the story:

> My brother George was the eldest in a family of nine. He was a talented school teacher and a great help to my parents. I remember the relief we all felt when we heard the Armistice was signed on November 11, 1918, and I remember the shock and anguish we all felt a week later when the station agent at Veteran brought that fateful telegram. The telegram said he was missing. Six months later, he was officially declared dead.
>
> It was about another year before we received his trunk. In that trunk was a receipt for a number of photographs he had taken just before he went to France from England. Mother wrote that photographer and he had kept the pictures. It was a wonderful photograph showing his "wings" and his official uniform. There were 12 copies of it — one for each of us. You can imagine how we have all cherished this remembrance.

Marjorie was such a loyal sister. When I visited her after receiving her letter, she told me again and again that, had George lived, he would have been the Minister of Education for the Alberta government. She was sure of it. He was that talented and that capable and that beloved by his sister. No wonder she had to have his name in the family's midst.

∽

Wop May and Freddy McCall were two of the lucky ones: they lived through World War I, and they came out with their wings. In other words, they learned how to fly a plane and went on to fame and fortune as a result. Well, fame at least. They were among the best known of a whole

120

breed of bush pilots that began to fly Canada's north country in the 1920s and 30s.

Wop May took his flight training in England. On his first flight into enemy territory, his squadron leader told him to stay out of the action, to watch from the sidelines so he'd know what to do another time. Wop May couldn't resist. He waded into the thick of things and fired his guns so repeatedly that they jammed. Suddenly he remembered his orders and headed for the sidelines, only to be noticed by the most famous German air ace of all, the dreaded Baron of Richtofen. Sensing a sure thing, the Baron chased him through the sky and would likely have caught the rookie whose guns had jammed except for one thing: squadron leader Roy Brown had also noticed May's predicament. Just as the Red Baron closed in for the kill, Roy Brown fired from above, and the German plane plunged to earth.

And so a legend was born. Wop May got the lion's share of the glory for bringing down the Red Baron because he stayed on in Edmonton after the war and continued to behave like a hero. Everything he did was larger than life. He flew mail and cargo where no one had flown mail and cargo before. He helped track down the Mad Trapper of Rat River in the Arctic, the first time that a plane had been used on a manhunt. In January of the following year, he and Vic Horner made a historic trip to Fort Vermilion with diphtheria antitoxin. Just to make the trip about as impossible as possible, they had to fly in an open cockpit Avro Avian biplane. Incredibly, they made it in two days, and when they returned to Edmonton, they were greeted at the airport as the conquering heroes that they were. Northern communities had been isolated until then, and when disease or accident touched them, they had to cope or die. Suddenly and dramatically, the air age changed all that.

For Wop May, the next twenty years weren't quite as exciting as the first years in the industry, so one day he decided to try a different kind of climbing. He went mountain climbing in Utah and died of a heart attack. He was fifty-seven. His gravemarker in the Edmonton Cemetery doesn't even hint at his interesting life.

Freddy McCall took up barnstorming when he returned from World War I. He went from town to town with his airplane and did crazy tricks in the sky. Once he had the attention of the townsfolk, he would land in a nearby field and sell rides. As a business, his was a sure bet. Flight was so new that most people wanted to try it, but there weren't enough people or enough sunny days in Alberta to keep McCall in business or in airplanes. Then there was the Stampede incident. He took the young sons of the Stampede manager up for a quick spin one day when suddenly the engine quit right over the busy Stampede grounds below. What to do — land on the track, which was busy with events, or land on a midway thronged with people? He decided on the midway, or else the plane did, but the results were miraculous. Like an awkward, over-sized butterfly, the plane came to a shuddering stop on top of the canvas roof of the merry-go-round. No one was injured, and rather than have a nervous breakdown, Freddy McCall decided to sell off pieces of the wrecked machine in order to make a bit of money. He may have been down, but he wasn't out.

McCall's chutzpah was legendary. On one occasion, he buzzed motorists on the old Banff-Calgary highway and had lots of fun until he flew straight into a haystack that some farmer had left inconsiderately close to the highway. Undaunted, he brushed himself off and hitched a ride back to the city — presumably with a motorist who had not been pestered earlier.

His biggest triumph was no joke. In 1929, he was asked to pilot a load of nitroglycerin from Shelby, Montana, to Calgary, where it would be transported by truck to Turner Valley and used for "shooting" an oil well that stubbornly refused to come in. The liquid nitroglycerin was packed in cans, but it remained an unstable and dangerous commodity. People assembled at the airport to watch the plane land, half expecting to see the explosion of a lifetime, but McCall's luck held. He landed safely, bumped over the grass and rocks on the so-called runway, and saw the load transferred to the next stage of its journey. It was only then that he realized the plane was out of gas. The engine wouldn't even turn over for him and it had to be towed to its hangar. Safe by a second or two.

McCall stayed in the air one way or another until he died in 1949, and even then his name remained. The Calgary airfield became McCall Field in 1953, but his gravemarker is so silent as to be invisible. It's in one of the long lines of Legion markers in the Calgary Burnsland Cemetery.

∼

I did not at first find many references to the Victoria Cross in Alberta's graveyards, but that's because, once again, we say less rather than more on our gravemarkers. We certainly can't be accused of the sin of pride in this part of the world. However, once I began asking questions, I found ten Victoria Cross winners that have some claim on Alberta. They're not all buried here, but part of their story is here, and each story is so remarkable, I couldn't resist them.

The Victoria Cross is a medal for valour in the face of the enemy, and until it was replaced by Canada's own Cross of Valour, it was the highest military decoration that a fighting man could receive. It was Queen Victoria's idea in 1856, and since that time 136 Canadians have been given the award.

The only Victoria Cross winner who was actually born in Alberta was Ian Bazalgette, born in Calgary in 1918. He and his family returned to their native England when young Bazalgette was still in school, so there wasn't anything Canadian about his war service with the Royal Air Force. Still, Alberta knows a good thing when it sees it, and Alberta claims him.

On a bombing mission over France, Bazalgette's Lancaster plane was hit badly, but he managed to keep it under control long enough to complete the bombing assignment. Various parts of the plane were in flames by then. Two of the crew members were injured. Bazalgette ordered the remaining crew members to parachute to safety, then tried to land the plane so that the injured could be rescued. He almost managed, but a moment after landing, the plane exploded. Bazalgette was buried in a village churchyard near the site of the crash. He was twenty-six years old, the only Alberta connection to get his VC in the Second World War.

Eight of the remaining Alberta connections received their medals for action in the First World War.

John Chipman Kerr was born in Nova Scotia but was homesteading near Spirit River when the First World War broke out. He and his brother set out immediately for Edmonton to enlist, leaving behind a sign on their shack door which read, "War is hell but what is homesteading?" He got his VC for an incredible piece of derring-do that involved a one-man capture of prisoners and a significant advance upon the enemy. On his return to Canada, he moved to British Columbia and is buried at Port Moody.

Cecil John Kinross came to Canada as a young man and homesteaded in the Lougheed area. The action that won him the VC was right out of Hollywood — he advanced alone in broad daylight on an enemy machine gun emplacement, killed the crew of six, and destroyed the gun. Somehow he lived to tell the tale and at the end of the war came home to his farm at Lougheed. The Legion there is named for him, and he's buried in the local cemetery.

Alex Brereton signed up for the First World War in Manitoba but came to a farm near Elnora after the war. Like Kinross, he was awarded his VC for removing the crew of a machine gun emplacement, having inspired other soldiers to charge and capture five remaining machine gun positions. He is buried in Elnora.

Raphael Zengel also destroyed a machine gun emplacement and killed the enemy crew. After the war, he homesteaded near Rocky Mountain House. He donated his medals to the local Legion before he died and asked them to scatter his remains on the Field of Honour. They did, and they also put up two of the most handsome war memorials in Alberta, both dedicated to Zengel's memory.

James Peter Robertson was born in the Maritimes but came to Medicine Hat in 1899, where he worked with the CPR until he joined up in 1915. In the terrible conflict at Passchendaele in Belgium, Robertson rushed a machine gun and crew. He survived the rush but was killed later the same day when he tried to bring a wounded soldier to the safety of a nearby trench. He is buried near the battle site.

Harcus Strachan was a soldier most of his life. He came to Canada from Scotland in 1908 and served with Canadian forces in the First World War. His VC came about because his squadron leader was killed and he took command, leading a most effective charge on the enemy. When he returned to Canada, Strachan served with various military reserve units in Edmonton and southern Alberta and then went back into the thick of things when World War II came along. He moved to Vancouver when he retired and is buried there.

Frederick Maurice Watson Harvey was Irish by birth but Canadian by choice. He earned his VC in World War I when he singlehandedly attacked a machine gun emplacement and put it and the men operating it out of commission. In fact, most of the VC winners seem to have tackled machine guns. Considering the damage that a machine gun could inflict on one human body, this was a demonstration of courage that no one could deny. In the Second World War, Harvey was District Officer Commanding for Alberta. He died in Calgary and is buried in Fort Macleod.

George Pearkes, perhaps the best-known of all the Alberta-connected VC winners, was born in England but came to Canada to be part of the Berkhamsted Farm school in Red Deer, an early version of an agricultural college, where he was supposed to learn how to be a Canadian farmer. After two years at the school, he took a homestead in the Clearwater area west of Red Deer, but he couldn't make any money at it, so he joined the army instead. Military life apparently suited him better than farming, because he never went back to it, staying instead in the military between the wars and throughout the Second World War as well. Once he had won almost every military honour that he could, he became a politician, first an MP and eventually the lieutenant-governor for British Columbia. He is buried in the country churchyard next to the Holy Trinity Anglican Church in West Saanich on Vancouver Island.

Hampden Zane Churchill Cockburn received his VC during the Boer War, when he and a small group of men held off an enemy attack long enough to allow their guns and other equipment to be moved out of danger. All but Cockburn were killed in the action. How anything in peacetime could be as dangerous as that is hard to imagine, but Cockburn was killed by a wild horse on his ranch in Graburn Gap in 1913. The notice in the *Medicine Hat News* reported that his mother back in Toronto was prostrated in her room over the awful news and "the relief of tears is denied her." I haven't found out exactly where he is buried, but I would guess with other members of the Cockburn family in Toronto.

And finally, Alberta had a Victoria Cross all by itself — its owner unknown. In the spring of 1987, a woman brought an old suitcase full of what she thought was mostly junk — old war medals and such — to Red Deer auctioneer Bud Haynes to see if he thought it might be worth something. He took one look and knew she had a treasure trove. One of the medals was a Victoria Cross awarded in 1858 to a British naval officer named Dr. George Bell Chicken. Nobody knows how the medal made its way to Canada and into an old suitcase in Alberta, but there it was, and it was undoubtedly valuable. Once the word got out, Haynes received interested calls from all over the world. In addition to the VC, the suitcase contained three War of 1812 general service awards, a series of awards from the North West Rebellion, and other international military medals. It was a great find and a great coup for a western Canadian auction house.

That particular Victoria Cross continued its mysterious ways. It was bought the night of the auction by an unidentified man who paid his $95,000 and left before people could find out anything about him. The other medals brought another $42,000, not a bad night's work for an old suitcase. In fact, even the suitcase was sold — for $30.

~

The First and Second World Wars touched Canadian lives but not Canadian soil, except for the Prisoner of War camps that were established across the country. Enemies captured in the course of fighting had to be confined somewhere, and Canada had to do its part in this unhappy task. About 30,000 men, mostly from Germany and Italy, lived in thirty-six different Canadian locations for a while during the two wars. Some of them died here as well, which means that we had POW sections in some of our graveyards.

Alberta had the largest camps in Canada during the Second World War: one in the mountains at Kananaskis; a temporary camp near Seebe, also in the mountains; two large camps at Medicine Hat and Lethbridge, and a smaller one for officers at Wainwright. It was the camp at Medicine Hat that gained the broadest reputation, mostly because of the two brutal murders that took place there. The trials that followed were widely reported all over the country.

August Plaszek was murdered in the summer of 1943 by some of his fellow POWs who thought he was a traitor to Nazi principles. Three men were tried for the crime but only one hanged, Werner Schwalb, and he was apparently unrepentant to the end. When he was led to the gallows, he said, "My Fuhrer, I follow thee."

Then, in the fall of 1944, a quiet, bookish POW who translated Canadian newspapers for his fellow prisoners was murdered, partly, it is thought, because the other prisoners refused to believe the news coming from the front. According to what Dr. Karl Lehmann was reading, their side was losing the war, and since that couldn't be happening, they decided to kill the messenger. There was also plenty of intrigue in the camp about who was a traitor and who wasn't, and somehow Dr. Lehmann got caught in the crossfire. Four men were found guilty of his murder, and all four were hanged in the yard of the Lethbridge jail on December 18, 1946.

They were all buried in the jail yard. Other prisoners of war who died of disease, accident, suicide, or attempted escape were buried in the community graveyards closest to their camps. In the end, Medicine Hat had eighteen buried in the Hillside Cemetery, Lethbridge had seventeen, Queen's Park in Calgary had five, and Wainwright had one.

But it takes a mother to put war into perspective. Sometime in the 1950s, the mother of one of the young men buried in Medicine Hat came to Canada to check on her boy. She stayed for two weeks, visiting the graveyard every day, putting flowers on all the POW graves, reblacking the lettering on the markers. She had to see for herself where her son lay. Just because he happened to end up on the wrong side during the war didn't mean he wasn't loved, wasn't missed in other lives. In May of 1971, when the German War Graves Commission relocated all POW graves across Canada to one central location in the Woodland Cemetery in Kitchener, Ontario, she was there for the dedication ceremony. Once more with feeling.

∽

THE LAST WORD: On the marker of an unidentified Canadian soldier buried at Normandy, June 6, 1944, are the words:

> *He loved the simple things,*
> *He hated war,*
> *But when his call came,*
> *He gave his all.*

∽

Stories That Confound

Someday we'll understand

...epitaph on the grave of Durrant Verner Dunlop
in the Canmore graveyard, killed at Lethbridge, 1943

Death is the biggest mystery of all, and graveyards are thought to be spooky, strange, and frightening because they are the repository of this great unknown. I've seen it happen again and again. I'll tell someone that I'm writing a book about graveyards, and the conversation screeches to a halt. There's a long pause while I get checked over for signs of strange behaviour, and I have to hasten to reassure my listeners that I am OK, that I simply use the graveyard as a source of interesting stories. And then I try to defuse the situation further by bringing the conversation around to the little mysteries that I've found in graveyards. Mysteries that we can solve, and therein lies a lot of fun. For instance, just how would a "survivor" of General Custer end up in the Three Hills Cemetery?

That was one of my best mysteries.

There is a small white marble marker on the edge of the Three Hills Cemetery that states matter-of-factly: **John McAlpine, 1849-1941, The Last Survivor of General Custer.** That last line leaves several mysteries in its wake, not the least of which is the word "survivor." According to historical accounts of Custer's Last Stand, there were no survivors. And even if there were, how did this one end up in a graveyard in Three Hills, Alberta?

I started my search for answers in various Three Hills history books. No luck. No luck, either, with the first few phone calls I made. Nobody seemed to know anything about John McAlpine. So I decided to work from the other end of the story and wrote off to the National Park Service at the Little Bighorn Battlefield National Monument in Montana.

According to their records, McAlpine was not listed with the 7th Cavalry at the Battle of the Little Bighorn in 1876. They suggested I

128

check further with the Military Service Archives in Washington. So I wrote another letter, and from them I learned that a John McAlpine had indeed enlisted in Boston, Massachusetts, on May 5, 1875, and had served in troops "D" and "G" of the 7th Cavalry; however, they couldn't find any specific connection to the battle at Little Bighorn. "Nevertheless," they wrote, "he served under Custer."

Their detailed answer included a copy of the oath of enlistment and allegiance that John McAlpine had signed in 1875 when he joined up. According to this document, he was born in Ayrshire, Scotland; he was by occupation a clerk, and he agreed to serve the United States of America "honestly and faithfully against all their enemies or opposers whomsoever" for a period of five years. It was all very interesting, except that the original questions remained: how did McAlpine become a "survivor" and how did he end up in Three Hills?

The answers finally came courtesy Ralph Loosmore, an old-timer of the Sunnyslope district south of Three Hills. Loosmore actually remembered John McAlpine, and what he didn't remember, he told me to check out in the history book of the Sunnyslope district. Sure enough, the whole story was there, an interview with McAlpine himself reported in the *Calgary Herald* in 1938, three years before his death at the ripe old age of ninety-two.

By his own account, McAlpine was at Little Bighorn, but he was two days late for the big battle. He and approximately sixty other soldiers were in charge of supply wagons, and they got held up by rough terrain and swollen streams. When they finally caught up with the rest of their regiment, they found nothing but bodies, fellow soldiers killed by Sitting Bull and his warriors. History books say it was 225 men dead; McAlpine put the toll at 317. And contrary to every other account of the battle, McAlpine maintained it wasn't a total massacre. One man did make it out alive, he said, a Metis scout who pulled a Sioux blanket from one of the dead Indians, wrapped himself in it and escaped. McAlpine said he knew the scout personally and had talked to him after the battle, but in 1938, some sixty-two years later, he couldn't remember the man's name.

In 1901, John McAlpine moved to a homestead in the Sunnyslope district of what would become Alberta. And that's how he ended up in the Three Hills Cemetery. Mystery solved, although it sure would be interesting to find out about that other survivor!

~

Speaking of surviving, the Peace River country was no picnic in the very early days. Survival was a constant struggle, which is why it seemed exceeding strange to find that Torquil McLeod had apparently survived his stay in the North so well that he had two burial sites.

This was another good mystery.

In the summer of 1991, I travelled with Aurelia Vangrud and Reverend J. Hoskin, both Peace River history buffs, to the site of two long since abandoned missions on Buffalo Bay, an arm of Lesser Slave Lake near Grouard. Mrs. Vangrud found rhubarb holding its own among native grasses on a flat piece of land on the lake's edge — a sure sign of the once-upon-a-time mission — and Rev. Hoskin and I found remnants of both the Catholic and Anglican cemeteries on the bluff above the bay. Both cemeteries had more or less returned to the wild, but on the edge of the Anglican cemetery, in the midst of all this riotous growth, was one mysterious brand-new grave, perfectly straight, properly fenced, and meticulously tidy. It belonged to Torquil MacLeod, who died in 1915.

Because the gravemarker had the RCMP symbol on it, I wrote the police station nearest the old Grouard site and asked them about the Torquil MacLeod grave. I figured there had to be a story to this one. The Staff Sergeant at High Prairie responded promptly, telling me that RCMP detachments must look after any "remote" or "abandoned" gravesites of RCMP or NWMP members in their area. Someone had come to them a few years earlier and told them about Constable MacLeod's grave in the old cemetery, and since the cemetery was falling to pieces, shouldn't they do something about it? So they did. They ordered a new headstone, covered the grave with a concrete cap, constructed a fence that would discourage the most determined cow, and congratulated themselves on doing their duty.

Mystery solved, or so I thought until later that summer when I found another Torquil McLeod, this time in the Fort Macleod Cemetery. Torquil being the uncommon name that it is, I checked my information later and found that the two markers were almost identical, almost but not quite. That's when I wrote off to the RCMP Archives in Ottawa to see if they could solve the mystery of the MacLeods/McLeods/Macleods. They told me that Torquil McLeod was a member of the NWMP in the Grouard

130

area when he died in 1913. At that time, he was buried in the Anglican cemetery at the mission. However, when RCMP officials learned that the old mission graveyard was not going to be maintained, they moved the grave to the special NWMP section in the Fort Macleod Cemetery in 1971. Somehow that information did not remain on file at the High Prairie detachment, which is why they responded to the local complaint with a whole new headstone, fence, the works. All of this for an empty grave.

Besides marking an empty grave, they also spelled the name wrong (it is McLeod); they gave him the wrong regimental number and the wrong number of years served, and they even put him in the wrong service. Torquil McLeod was NWMP, not RCMP. Unfortunately the lovely new grave in the old mission graveyard will have to go, I am told, although it still remained in the summer of 1993, two years after the initial discovery.

~

Torquil McLeod likely spent some of his NWMP years looking for Ernest Cashel. Most police in those days did, because Ernest Cashel was at various times Alberta's most wanted criminal. Even to this day, he is arguably the province's most famous criminal, but do you think I could find his grave? No way. It was as if he had disappeared into thin air, and it made me wonder about other men and women who had found themselves on the wrong side of the law. Where are they buried? What does it say on their gravemarkers? The more I wondered and the more I searched, the more mysteries I discovered.

Ernest Cashel arrived in central Alberta in 1901, a hardened criminal who had escaped from at least two prisons and a variety of charges in the United States. On the lam in Canada, he didn't seem to have mended his ways. Within a year, he was arrested in Ponoka for cashing worthless cheques and put on a train for Calgary, where he was expected to repent in jail for awhile. Instead, he told his captors he had to go to the bathroom, then he slipped out through the train window.

Cashel stayed out of sight for awhile, but when a farmer in the Ponoka district was killed, police started looking for him again. This time they caught him and managed to hold on to him long enough to bring him to trial for murder. The trial took nine days, the jury took thirty-five minutes, and the judge took two minutes to decide the outcome: Cashel was guilty and would hang.

If it had ended there, that a guilty man died for his crimes, then Cashel's case would have been buried and forgotten. But Cashel wasn't done yet. His brother John happened along for a visit two weeks before Ernest's scheduled hanging, and that night, Ernest surprised his guard by pointing two loaded revolvers right at him. He was on the loose again.

The whole province went into shock. Cashel had already proved that he was light on his feet and might appear anywhere on the map, so a total of forty men were put on the chase. Even so, it took them six weeks to track him down. When they finally found him, he was in a cellar beneath an old bunkhouse on a farm about seven miles east of Calgary. He'd been in the area all the time, reading about himself in the *Calgary Daily Herald* and generally enjoying his fifteen minutes of fame.

Once back in jail, he was watched around the clock. Only his lawyer, the famous Paddy Nolan, and Rev. George Kerby were allowed as visitors. Nolan tried various legal appeals, but nothing worked. It was left to Kerby to prepare the young man for his fate, in the course of which Cashel agreed to write a bit of advice for other young men who might be tempted to break the law. "Take my advice, dear boys, and stay at home, shun novels, bad company and cigarettes," he wrote the day before he was hanged. "Don't do anything, boys, you are afraid to let your mother know."

Rev. Kerby stayed with Cashel through the grisly climb to the platform, stood by as the noose was tightened, and said "The Lord's Prayer" as the dirty deed was done.

And that's where most of the accounts of Cashel end, with the hanging. No one ever mentions the burial. When hanging was the acceptable form of ultimate punishment, the bodies of the hanged men were often buried in lime on the prison grounds immediately after the nasty business. Sometimes they were moved later, but most often they weren't. Anyway, that was not Cashel's end. According to the *Calgary Daily Herald,* his body was placed in a coffin and taken by the undertaker to the potter's field at Union Cemetery. A potter's field is the area in a graveyard designated in earlier times for the burial of people without friends or funds. Ernest Cashel was buried with them without ceremony and without a marker to his memory.

∾

The story surrounding Emilio Picariello's grave is more mysterious than Cashel's, but then Picariello was a law breaker of a different sort. In many ways, he was a thoroughly good guy — a devoted family man and a respected member of the community who came to the Crowsnest area in 1911 and began a legitimate hotel operation. Once he could see the profits to be made in the import of liquor, illegal though it may have been, he moved into rum running, as the commerce was then known. He'd bring the stuff in from British Columbia or Montana and resell it to Alberta and Saskatchewan customers. He had to get more and more clever to outwit the police — rigging up cars with specially designed hiding places, arranging informants who would warn him about surprise police raids and roadblocks, making sure he had faster cars than the police — and most of the time, he was remarkably successful. Even the most law-abiding in his midst had to admire his chutzpah. But things got out of control one afternoon in 1922 when Picariello heard that his son Steve had been killed at a police roadblock. Without checking the facts, he grabbed two revolvers, handed one to Florence Lassandro, the wife of one of his employees, and the pair roared off to deliver justice, Picariello-style.

The first policeman that they met, Steve Lawson at the Alberta Provincial Police headquarters in Coleman, couldn't seem to make Pick understand that his son wasn't dead at all, he had only been injured. There was some pushing and shoving, and somehow one of the revolvers went off, killing Lawson on the spot. Even now, no one is sure just who pulled the trigger. It might have been Pick, but it could also have been Lassandro.

If Picariello had elected to a trial separate from Florence Lassandro's, the outcome might have been different; however, just because he was a famous rum runner, a man who thumbed his nose at law and order, didn't mean Picariello wasn't a gentleman. He was with Florence Lassandro when the policeman was killed. They had both intended revenge. What did it matter who fired the fatal shot? The fact that revenge was unnecessary only added to the drama.

The court case made headlines all over Canada for weeks and it made the Crowsnest Pass sound like the epitome of the Wild West. In fact, the Crowsnest was a nice quiet area, peopled by nice quiet folk, a lot of whom liked the "Pick" because he kept things lively, employed a fair number of locals, and was generous with his money. But popularity was not enough

— Picariello and Lassandro were hanged at Fort Saskatchewan jail on May 3, 1923.

And then what happened? The people at the Frank Slide Interpretive Centre know just about everything there is to know about the history of the Crowsnest area, but they had no idea what had become of the bodies of their two most famous residents. All the accounts I read ended with the hanging, as if that were the end of the story.

But it wasn't the end, at least not according to Bill Connelly, Sr. of the firm of Connelly McKinley in Edmonton, undertakers there since the turn of the century. He alone knows the whereabouts of the "Pick," and he says that's how it will be until he dies. Then his son will be authorized to tell the rest of us.

Connelly says that Picariello was originally buried in the jail graveyard at Fort Saskatchewan. Some years ago, there was talk in the Crowsnest Pass about bringing his body back and perhaps erecting a cairn, making a bit of a hero out of him. The Alberta government got wind of this and didn't like the idea of lionizing a known criminal, so they quietly asked Connelly to move Picariello and Lassandro to a spot known only to him, which he did.

I protested to Mr. Connelly that someone in the government must know where they are. But when he suggested I try the Solicitor General's department, he smiled as if he knew the hopelessness of tracing such an obscure detail through government channels. So, there you are. Only one person in Alberta knows where the "Pick" and Lassandro are buried, and that person is not telling.

~

Many of the hangings in Alberta's early years took place at the jail in Fort Saskatchewan, and many of the burials were held in the cemetery behind the original jail buildings. The jail itself has been moved to a new location, but the old cemetery remains, a rather forlorn piece of history in a weed-choked piece of land alongside the river. There are eighteen white metal crosses still standing there, still more or less in two straight lines as you might expect in a jail setting. But there are no names on the crosses; they are completely silent. It's that lack of names that puzzled me. Were there names once upon a time and has nature erased them? Or were these men buried without the benefit of names?

Answers to all the puzzles presented by the little graveyard are hard to come by. It is known that there were twenty-nine hangings at the Fort Saskatchewan jail between 1916 and 1960. Not all of the condemned men were buried at the jail, only the ones who were not claimed by families. Other prisoners died in jail of natural causes, and if no one came to claim them, they too were put in the jail's cemetery. Thus, the cemetery is the resting place for eighteen people that nobody wanted, but why aren't they at least named? It seemed to me that information would surely be available. But apparently it isn't. Various historians and researchers through the years have tried to determine just who is buried there, but all records seem to be lost. The Solicitor General's department has no information, they say, and neither does the Provincial Archives, which means that the Fort Saskatchewan jail cemetery is a cemetery of unknowns in more ways than one.

The one fact that the old cemetery does tell, loud and clear, is that we treated our prisoners differently in the first part of this century. We hanged them, for one thing, and we didn't worry about their rights as human beings. That being the case, maybe the cemetery should stay as it is. There is talk of prettying it up with an iron fence and interpretive panels and such, but it can never tell the bleak story as well as it does right now.

~

As for the women who found themselves on the wrong side of the law, well, they are even more invisible in the graveyard. Women who committed lesser crimes like prostitution and running a public house are no different than Florence Lassandro, who lies unmarked and unknown to all but one. They, too, seem to have disappeared.

Pearl Miller was Calgary's most famous madam, having run houses of prostitution in at least three different locations in the city during the course of her career. Toward the end of that career, she repented of her sinful ways and got religion. But do you think I can find her? James Gray who wrote *Red Lights on the Prairies*, the definitive book on prostitution in the West, told me she had died in Calgary in 1957 and that her name was really Pearl Rose. I've checked the city and district cemeteries, but they have no record of Pearl as a Miller or a Rose. How could this most famous of Calgary characters just vanish like that?

Two equally well-known ladies from the Drumheller area, Mary

Roper and Fanny Ramsley, operated substantial houses outside the town limits. The stories about them are legion. It is said that there used to be such line-ups that the men from the night shift would still be waiting in line when the men from the day shift arrived. Drumheller was a mining town, after all, and for a while the ratio of men to women in the valley was higher than anywhere else in the West. Prostitution seemed a logical service in such circumstances, and Mary and Fanny provided it with class — not, of course, that they took an active part in the business. They were already older and fairly well fixed when they arrived in Drumheller, so they served as hostess and manager of what might be called "social clubs." Their establishments offered music, fine dining, and conversation along with other more traditional services. The "law" never harassed them the way they did Pearl Miller in Calgary; they were out of town and outside police jurisdiction. But the Depression of the 1930s hit them the same as it did other businesses, and they just sort of disappeared from the scene.

So it's back to my everlasting question: where are they now? What happens to old prostitutes when the cheering stops?

Well, I found the answer for one of them. Mary Roper is buried in the Drumheller Cemetery under her own name. There's no mention of her rival, Fanny, even though the town's longtime doctor says she died in Drumheller too and should be buried in their midst. She might have used another name when it came time to die.

∾

Captain Shott answered to several names and was famous by whatever name you called him, but come 1991 when I wanted to find his grave, I couldn't. Once again, the mystery was "Where?"

The clerks at the Athabasca town hall agreed that he should be in their cemetery. One of his names, Louis Fassoneuve, was right there on their map, but when I looked for the grave in the cemetery, I couldn't find it. The town archivist, Marilyn Mol, and a longtime resident of Athabasca went out looking; they too found nothing. They think he is marked by a slight depression in the old part of the graveyard, but they can't be sure. Is that the way a legend ends?

Captain Shott was neither a captain nor a Shott. He got the name "Shott" because he was a good shot, and he was called "Captain" because he was a good river man. In fact, his name was Louis Fosseneuve or Louis Fassoneure or Louis Fassoneuve — take your pick. His descendants did: some called themselves Shott and some used Fosseneuve.

Names aside, he was the man who could get a scow from point A to point B no matter what, through rapids, low water, high water, portage, and storm. The Klondikers competed for his help, missionaries regularly sought his expertise, fur traders wanted him. He was strong, he knew the northern rivers, and he was well liked by men who worked for him. Every spring, he would show up in Athabasca Landing just before break-up and get himself some crews. For the rest of the summer, he would pilot loaded scows downstream to northern destinations, then walk back to Athabasca Landing to do it all over again. Not all of the loads got through — that was par for the course — and not all of the boatmen got through either. It was dangerous business, and the wooden crosses all along the watery routes were a constant reminder of that fact.

It was Captain Shott who first shot the Athabasca River's famous Grand Rapids, a treacherous piece of the river that falls some thirty feet in half a mile. The boatmen usually stopped before they reached the rapids, unloaded everything, and carried it around the falls to calmer waters below. It was time-consuming and a nuisance, and one day Captain Shott just couldn't stand the idea of portaging yet again. So he and his men took the scow down the falls successfully, load and all. According to a *Saturday Evening Post* article by Emerson Hough in March, 1914, this is how it happened:

> Louis Fassoneure's claim to remembrance is that when still a young man, tall and strong as a moose, he rebelled at the thought of a mile-and-a-half hill of portage and swore he would run the Grand Rapids of the Athabasca or perish.
>
> He ran the right hand channel and did not perish; came back and did it over again, exulting; took boat after boat through year after year — millions of dollars worth of cargo.

For sure, he was a hero if the *Saturday Evening Post* said so!

One May day when he was seventy-four years old and preparing for yet another season on the northern waterways, Captain Shott told an old friend that he was as fit as a fiddle and ready to hit the watery trails. The next day, he cut himself. Then blood poisoning set in, and in those pre-antibiotic days, nothing could save him. He died a few days later.

It was a grand funeral: the hearse was followed by the town band, civic officials, members of the family, and several hundred citizens in some twenty-one rigs. Oh yes, about 150 "breeds" were there as well — that's how the newspaper referred to the Metis who were present at the funeral to say goodbye to one of their own. Metis were dismissed in a similar way in most accounts of the life and times of western Canada in the early days, which may be why Captain Shott, a Metis, is marked in the local graveyard by a depression only. But there may be a happy post-script to this story. The town is now thinking of erecting a proper memorial for their Captain.

As it happens, I did find the name Fosseneuve in a graveyard, not in Athabasca but in Lac La Biche in the old mission cemetery. There I read on a small marble stone that David Fosseneuve died April, 1883, aged three years. It could have been a brother to Louis or a cousin or no relation at all, but I'll bet there was a connection. Western Canada was a small world in those days. Besides, Lac La Biche was a vital part of the earliest water transportation routes, a logical place for the Captain's beginnings.

~

Sometimes a gravemarker may pose a mystery in what it doesn't say; at other times, it becomes all the more mysterious because of what it does say. Take, for example, the plaque on the cairn for Dr. Greene, who was the dentist in Peace River for years. As far as town folks knew, he was just a guy who fixed their teeth, went hunting a lot, and occasionally flew to some sort of reunion in the United States. In other words, he was just regular folks. But when he died, a cairn in his memory was erected on the Peace River hills, and the plaque included the line: **"One of the first to fly."**

Well, that set the cat among the pigeons. The first to fly what? The first to fly where? What had this quiet man not told them? — Well, as it turns out, he hadn't told them just about everything about his first life.

Bill Greene grew up and went to university in the United States. He was about to hang up his shingle as a dentist when one day he found himself looking at scavenger buzzards, and that changed everything. From that moment on, he knew he wanted to fly, to be anywhere but on the ground. So he went to New York and watched the Wright brothers do-

138

ing glider experiments. Then he began drawing and building his own flying machines. Money was always a problem. He would just nicely get something built, and the thing would crash. In later years he said he had crashed as often as most people blow their noses.

Along with all the other aviators at the time, he experimented with different kinds of wings trying to achieve a smooth and straight ride, but he did not bother trying to make a sharp cutting edge on his wings. From his buzzard watching days, he knew that the cutting edge is not a decisive factor in flight. What it came down to, he decided, was the engine. You could make a wooden desk fly if you had enough engine power, he argued, and that's where the crunch came. He could not get reliable light engines for his prototypes.

Even so, he had a biplane that flew or "hopped" fairly well by 1906 or 1907, in which case he was the third man in the world to fly, right behind the Wright brothers and Glenn Curtiss. Another aviation historian made him the seventh to fly, so the truth probably lies somewhere in between. And that's what Dr. Greene never talked about in Peace River.

When he failed to make a commercially viable plane, he left the high flying, high finance world of aviation to move to the Peace River country. "Any place far from airplanes and worry," he said. And that's where he stayed, more or less. He headed off for a few years during the war to fly fighters, but once back in the North, he never flew his own plane again. He sometimes attended reunions of the "Early Birds of Aviation," a group of old fliers who had been in the air before 1915, but he could never be persuaded to give himself any credit in the aviation world. One reporter asked him what his greatest individual contribution was, and he responded, "Who can say what he, individually, was responsible for? Quite a number of men were making experiments and building machines about the same time. The basic principles of flight they arrived at remain, fundamentally, the same today."

Greene was much more willing to talk about the Peace River country. "It's a grand country," he told a reporter. "I can close up the office and go away for months with a tent, some grub and my gun. That's happiness." He and another Peace River old-timer, Norman Soars, persuaded the government to preserve a parcel of land up and down the valley from Peace River town for several miles. How he let them name it for him is hard to understand, what with his determination to be invisible, but the area is called the Greene Valley Game Preserve. It's the wooded area just south of his cairn. And it's where his ashes were scattered after his death in 1952 — from a plane, of course.

~

"By the way," a friend said to me one day, "did you know that Jesse James is buried in Stettler?"

"The real one?" I said. "You're kidding."

"All I know," she said, "is that someone told me Jesse James is in Stettler."

A few days later, I was talking to Ches Pye at Remco Memorials in Red Deer. He has been all over central Alberta installing tombstones so I said casually, "I hear that Jesse James is in Stettler." I expected him to scoff and explain away yet another graveyard myth, but without missing a beat, he said, "Nope, Jesse James is in Delburne."

So naturally I went to Delburne and right at the front of the graveyard is a gravemarker that very clearly says, "**Jesse James, At Rest.**" Right spelling and everything, except that this Jesse James died in 1957 and is buried next to his wife, Bessie. So much for that mystery. The Missouri Jesse died in a blaze of gunfire at the age of thirty-five, but our Jesse lived a long and useful life — virtue, of course, having its own rewards.

When I lamented to Michael Dawe at the Red Deer Museum and Archives that we really weren't very interesting people — our Jesse James turns out to be a nice guy — he handed me the file on James Gadsby. Shut me right up.

James Gadsby never talked much about his early days. The story was finally told by his daughter Anna, but not until she was in her nineties and living in a nursing home in Ponoka. Sensing that there was a bit of shame in some of Gadsby's memories, the family had never pushed for details. They just knew he had been a gunman and that now and then he dropped the name Jesse James. That's all he would say, but they could see he was an excellent marksman. It followed that he might have been an outlaw. Also, several members of the family who remembered that their dad had buried some guns in the farmyard went looking for them years later. With the help of metal detectors, they turned up a Colt .44 and Webley .45, just the sort of thing that outlaws would have used back in Jesse James' heyday.

Gadsby did tell his family that he was being pursued by a posse when he decided it might be a good idea to move to Canada. He took up land north of Mirror, settled down with a wife, Mary, and raised a family. The gravemarker he shares with Mary in the Mirror Cemetery makes no mention of his interesting youth, but it's a reminder that there may be more than meets the eye in a mild-mannered Albertan.

~

THE LAST WORD: On a small metal marker in the Innisfail Cemetery for John Penikett, died September 18, 1901, is an expression of the ultimate mystery:

Reader, where will you spend eternity?

~

Three Hills Cemetery

Stories Of Change

All that which pleases is for a moment.
All that which troubles is for a moment.
That only is important which is eternal.

...epitaph on gravemarker for Bertram Turner
Banister, in the Davisburg Cemetery near Calgary

You wouldn't normally think of a graveyard as reading material for so-cial history, but it is. I didn't cotton onto this fact at first and sometimes wrote down epitaphs without the corresponding names and dates, not knowing that those epitaphs gave me only half the story. Put the words together with the dates, the names, the symbols used on the tombstone, the materials of which the tombstone is made, and you have a book. In other words, the tombstone by itself has its own voice and deserves its own place in a study of social history.

Through the years, the tombstone got smaller or bigger, it said more or less, it cost more or less, it cried out for meaning some or not at all. Like any other fashion, it had its seasons. But even as it changed right along with the rest of society, it didn't change as much. That's the first piece of social history to read in our graveyards. Everything is relative, and relatively speaking, tombstones have not changed as much as other parts of society. There isn't a car or a can opener that hasn't changed drastically in 100 years; yet tombstones within a graveyard have not changed that much. Why?

Well, that's the second piece of social history to read on the tomb-stone. For all our brains and scientific breakthroughs and trips to the moon, we have not yet been able to figure out death. We haven't a new language for death, so when it comes time to bury one another, we have to fall back on the old language, the language of symbol and religion and tradition. We go to a church or a synagogue, we sing hymns, we put seldom-used words on the graves of our loved ones, words like "In God

We Trust" or "Thy Kingdom Come." Lacking a new understanding, we use old understandings.

The cross is a perfect example. When the population was overwhelmingly Christian, it was the most popular symbol in our graveyards — not surprisingly, since it symbolized resurrection and eternal life for believers. However, it's still the most visible symbol out there among the rocks, even though sociologists tell us that less than fifteen per cent of the population admits to any sort of regular church attendance. Either there is a lingering need for some sort of eternal reassurance, or, if you want to take the cynic's view, the choice of a cross on a gravemarker is the modern way of hedging our bets. If Christianity is right and the cross does guarantee some sort of special dispensation, then why not have one? At the very least it can't hurt, and that's the mixed message of the symbol of the cross nowadays.

Crosses have thus become a religious rabbit's foot, and even as I say that, I can hear our ancestors spinning in their graves. To them, the cross was a powerful symbol that spoke absolutely of God's promise. To treat it as a fail-safe would be blasphemy — it still is blasphemy for many people — but that is what is happening.

Choosing a cross has also become a question of design rather than religion. One hundred years ago, the cross had very decided meanings in its various forms and could separate the sheep from the lambs in a cemetery in a minute (the Protestants from the Catholics, for example), but those differences have blurred. People now choose the cross they like from a tombstone catalogue, never mind denomination or religious affiliation. Thus, the Celtic cross is no longer the exclusive choice of people with British or Scottish background. The three-pronged cross is used by all and sundry, not just by people from Eastern Europe and so on. The need for meaning as expressed by a cross has never changed, but the choices have.

The cross is just one example of how things have changed and not changed within graveyards. Here are some others, as I observed them on my travels.

~

Before 1910 there weren't many formal graveyards in western Canada, which is proof that when it comes to traditions surrounding death and burial, the Indians of western Canada made the biggest changes of all. Before the white settlers came, Indians disposed of their dead in a variety of ways, depending on the circumstances and weather, but many of them employed a version of tree burials or platform burials. Bodies were wrapped and left on a high spot so that the spirits could easily enter the spirit world beyond. Theirs was the only distinctively "Canadian" or at the very least "North American" style of interment that came out of the West. An example of a tree burial still exists at Indian Cabins north of High Level in northern Alberta. Years ago, a child died and was enclosed in a hollowed out log, which was then placed in the branches of a tall poplar near the community. The tiny bundle is still there. This may be the only public example of the Indian tradition, but the man who took me to the Cluny Cemetery to see Chief Crowfoot's grave told me that Indians know where to find ancient burial sites where bodies were left on high ledges or hillsides to be closer to the ancestors. They just don't talk about them much for fear someone will want to change them. They've had enough change for awhile, he said.

The settlers who changed everything for the Indians did not change their own customs concerning burial when they got to this country. As the need arose, they established graveyards, and although they didn't look exactly like the ones at home, they sometimes came close. The rules were pretty straightforward: 1) A legal description of the land had to be sent to Regina, the NWT capital; 2) a company of at least twenty people had to be formed and registered to be responsible for the graveyard.

Even those brief rules were often ignored. After all, nobody in this brave new world intended to die. The settlers had come here to make a life for themselves; they certainly weren't about to set up a cemetery society before it was absolutely necessary. Indeed, some of the communities didn't have the twenty people necessary to form a company, so cemeteries were established when needed, and they operated with a minimum of fuss.

It was the death of one-year-old Edna Robb in 1889 that created the demand for a graveyard in the Pine Creek area. Her folks selected a corner of their own land and declared it to be the Pine Creek Cemetery. The paperwork was finished later, but first Edna was buried in the farthest corner of the designated area, the corner with the best view over the Pine Creek valley and the Rockies in the distance.

City graveyards started out the same way. The old Jewish cemetery in Calgary was established when ten-month-old Goldie Bell died on September 3, 1904. There was no synagogue in the city yet and no Jewish cemetery, but as small as it was, the community immediately sought a place for the child. Thus did the first piece of the Jewish cemetery come into being, the piece that is now closest to the west side of Macleod Trail.

The tombstones that were used in these brand-new cemeteries also carried on the traditions of the old country. When that tradition was British, and most were in the first years of Canadian settlement, the gravemarkers were cast in the Victorian mould; that is, they tended to be fairly substantial, they were made of sandstone or marble, and they were covered with Christian symbolism and words.

Cecil Hargrave's tombstone in the Hillcrest Cemetery in Medicine Hat contains all those elements — it's marble and fairly large for a child's grave, its design includes a rose, which stands for youth and purity or in some cases the Virgin Mary, and it concludes with a Bible verse: **"Of such is the Kingdom of Heaven."** Interestingly, it also includes the signature of the stone mason, R. Reid of Montreal, so we have some idea how far this marker had to come to mark young Cecil in 1886.

Biblical references and symbols marked almost all the tombstones back then. The gravemarker of William John Hankins Gould in the Hainstock Cemetery west of Olds is pitted with age, falling apart at the seams, but you can still see the lilies carved into the arch of the stone, the epitaph that accepts, **"Thy will be done."** George Murray's sandstone marker in the same vicinity is equally aged, but you can see lilies carved into the pedestal and a Bible verse: **"The Lord Giveth His Beloved Sleep."**

Catholics most often used the term **"Rest in Peace"** or the shortened "**RIP**" on their gravemarkers and incorporated the Latin cross into the design. The Latin cross is the one that looks like the cross upon which Christ was crucified, and in many Catholic graveyards you'll find the Latin cross with a figure of Christ hanging on it, otherwise known as a crucifix.

Eastern Orthodox adherents generally included the Eastern cross or the Orthodox cross on their gravemarkers. It's the cross that has three bars intersecting one vertical bar. The bottom bar is slanted because, according to Orthodox teachings, that was the footrest of Christ when he was on the cross. Orthodox graveyards also featured the botonee cross, what I call the frilly cross. It's a Latin cross except that the arms end in rounded knobs.

For all the religious words or symbolism on those first graves, they seldom mentioned the words "death" or "died," referring instead to sleeping or to travel. The epitaph for Alice G. Clauson in the Innisfail Cemetery managed to do both — avoid the word death and convey the idea of travel to a better place.

The mother gave in tears and pain
The flower she most did love
She knew she should find her again
In the fields of light above.

Alice Clauson died in 1906 at the age of "1 yr. 8 ms and 16 ds." That's another characteristic of graves in the early days — the ages were often spelled out to the day, especially for children.

Hudson's Bay trader Colin Fraser died in 1867, but that isn't what it says on his gravemarker in the Edmonton Cemetery. Fraser **"departed this life suddenly."** And Eric Grant McKay in the Calgary Union Cemetery **"joined the noble army of martyrs and entered into rest eternal"** on February 2, 1902. Death is denied altogether on the marker of Helen Agnes Embury, who died in 1910 at the age of two months. **"She is not dead but sleepeth,"** we are told.

∼

The decade between 1910 and 1920 was a tough one for western Canadians, what with World War I followed by the flu epidemic, accompanied at all times by the normal hazards of living on the frontier. It was just one dangerous thing after another. No wonder the Grindley family put **"Safe at Last"** on their son's tombstone in the Red Deer Cemetery. Apparently they had done everything they could to protect him while he was on earth, but it wasn't enough. Richard John Grindley died April 6, 1913, at the age of ten months. At least in Heaven, he could be safe.

Obviously a religious faith was still on call to make sense of death and to provide comfort for the living. In the Edmonton Cemetery is an elaborate marble statue of a barefoot child holding an armful of roses, in memory of Douglas Earl Davis, born April 1, 1913, died July 9, 1917.

Our darling has gone the angels to join
We miss his bright face and heavenly smiles
But God's will was done so we must prepare
To meet darling Douglas in heaven so fair.

People were still not saying the word "death." Douglas has **"gone the angels to join,"** and Giovanni Sartorio, who is buried in the Coleman graveyard, was "**taken from the affection of the wife and relatives while employed at the Beaver Mines of Alberta, Canada, the 17 day of March, 1913, at the age of 35 years."** However, by the end of that decade, it was no longer possible to avoid the word "death." The First World War wrote it everywhere, even on tombstones. In Calgary Burnsland, for example, is a tribute to Private Herbert C. Hickey, who was **"Killed in France, April 9, 1917."** No softening of the facts there.

Surprisingly, what we could now say about the war overseas, we couldn't say about the wars fought in our own back yard. When the flu epidemic hit in 1918, Muir Edwards, son of Dr. O.C. Edwards and Henrietta Muir Edwards, was a professor at the University of Alberta in Edmonton. He volunteered to work at the temporary hospital set up in Pembina Hall, one of the University buildings. You can guess the ending of the story: he died of the disease himself and is buried in Edmonton's Mount Pleasant Cemetery. On his marker are the words, **"Greater love hath no man than this: That a man lay down his life for his friends. John 15:13."**

That same Bible verse was often used on the tombstones of soldiers as well. It was a patriotic time, the years between 1910 and 1920, and that showed up in our graveyards, along with mostly Christian sentiments and symbols. There was a harder edge developing, however. We were moving into troubled economic times.

~

The 1920s were mixed up years for Albertans. Times were getting tough in the West. New settlers had no money to begin with; old settlers weren't making much. Those families who could afford a tombstone for their loved ones still depended mostly on Christian sentiments and understandings. But more and more, people couldn't afford any kind of permanent marker.

In the old St. Patrick's graveyard in Lethbridge, I found a pile of what looked to be abandoned gravemarkers near a tool shed. On the top of the heap was a fairly attractive one, white marble with roses and a cross worked into the design. It was in memory of Victoria Nichita, aged five months, sixteen days, died April 14, 1922. Under the vital statistics was the information, **"Erected by Grandmother."** That single fact told a lot about the 1920s. I'm guessing here, but I'll bet that Victoria's mother and father couldn't afford a tombstone for their child, so grandma came through. Then the family likely moved on — to find better land, to look for work, to provide for the children who were still living — and Victoria got left behind. It couldn't be helped. Life had to go on. Many years later, there is no one left to claim Victoria's gravemarker, so it rests on a pile beside the tool shed.

That was certainly a characteristic of the 1920s — life did have to go on, and dwelling upon one's losses was not encouraged. Billy Patrick was two years old when he wandered away from his home on the banks of the Red Deer River in Drumheller and was never seen again. It was presumed that he had drowned. The river was close, and the hired girl had taken her eyes off him for just a minute. Besides, the family's faithful old dog was wet; it had to be a drowning.

The Patricks owned the Atlas Coal Mines in the Drumheller Valley. When they first heard their child had disappeared, Mr. Patrick said to his wife, "Don't make a fuss now." Public mourning just wasn't done in those days, so Mrs. Patrick kept a stiff upper lip, as was proper. But she told me in 1991, sixty-three years after the death of her child, that she thought of Billy every day and named him in her prayers every night.

It seems almost cruel, that idea that mourning should be a quiet, private affair and that life must go on as if nothing had happened. But maybe it was the best advice for the time. Terrible things did happen, and life did have to go on. No wonder the epitaph **"Gone But Not Forgotten"** became so popular.

Some people who died in those years were both gone and forgotten; they lived such solitary, isolated lives. One lovely summer's day, I went along with my brothers on their annual pasture tour, a wonderful excuse for the farmers in the area to get together, enjoy the day, and check on their cattle in the remote community pasture at the same time. We picked a spot at random for lunch, a piece of open meadow, and it was there that one of the men found a wooden cross marking what we had to assume was a grave. Nobody knew who it could have been, but there was some talk of an old trapper who had lived in the area way back in the 1920s. Guy always lived alone, or so the talk went. But if he lived alone, who put up the cross? Conversation drifted onto other matters eventually — cows, for one thing — but it struck me that this is another way that people's lives were marked when neither money nor community was available.

Graveyards in the 1920s were still not particularly well organized. While cities like Calgary had parks departments that looked after the maintenance of the city graveyards, smaller centres had to depend on the energy and goodwill of the community, which meant that some graveyards fared better than others, to put it mildly. Gadsby was one of the lucky ones. Its graveyard was adopted by a go-getting bunch of women known as the Omega Circle, a group that had been formed during the First World War to make money for soldiers overseas. The women enjoyed their association so much that they decided to stay together after the war and work within their own community. That's when they took on the care of the graveyard, and it made all the difference.

In this era, too, folks were leaving hints for the next generation. This is what August Link told us on his tombstone in the Century Meadows Baptist Church Cemetery near Camrose. How did he know the Dirty Thirties were right ahead?

What I used, that I had
What I saved, that I lost
What I bestowed, I still have.

∼

The decade between 1930 and 1940 shaped and affected lives for the next two generations. My mother, for instance, still can't throw anything away. "We might need that in case there's another Depression," she'll say when it comes time to clean out a closet or a cupboard. But do you think I could find one mention of the Depression or the Dirty Thirties in our graveyards? Not on your life.

No one admits to having died from The Great Depression, although lots did. At least, they died from causes related to the Depression: diseases and injuries that couldn't be treated for lack of money and resources, suicide brought on by despair, deaths in childbirth and childhood that might have been prevented with better food, better hygiene. Take the homemade concrete gravemarker of A. Richter in the Beiseker St. Mary's Cemetery that simply says **"Born and Died June, 1936."** Obviously this was a child who didn't live longer than a few days. Could the Depression have been a contributing factor? We're not told.

Actually, the chief indicator of the 1930s in our graveyards is the lack of indicators. Many of those who died in the period were buried without markers, or else they were buried beneath wooden markers that gradually rotted away. Sometimes families came back years later with a brand new marker and fulfilled an obligation they had carried with them for many years. Occasionally they couldn't find the exact location of the grave. That's why a fair amount of guessing went on in a lot of grave-yards, rural ones in particular, as to who was buried where.

The markers that do exist for the 1930s continue in the mostly Chris-tian vein, although here and there are signs of a more secular society. The grave of Luigi Fumagalli, 1897-1935, in the Hillcrest Cemetery, for example, doesn't make any Christian connections in its expression of grief:

We knew no sorrow, knew no grief
Till thy bright face was missed.

It does, however, include a stylized lily and a cross in its design, so Chris-tian roots are not entirely left out.

Amelia Muir, aunt to the young professor who died of the flu, has on her gravemarker in Fort Macleod: **"She served her day and genera-tion."** That's staying pretty close to earth. **"Her sun is gone dark/ While it was yet day,"** are the words on the gravemarker of Lillian Alice Herman, who died in 1935 and is buried in the Vulcan Cemetery. And the most neutral of all, the single most popular epitaph in Alberta, began appear-ing in the 1930s: **Ever Loved Ever Remembered**

~

The 1940s brought another war to the world. Since most of the men and women who died in action were buried overseas, our graveyards did not have to get bigger to accommodate those who were killed in action, but they did have to expand to hold those who came home to die. Walk

150

through a Field of Honour and see how many men died in 1942 and 1943, many as a result of the action in Dieppe, or in 1945 and 1946, as a result of wounds they brought home. The markers don't say much by themselves, but taken together they tell a lot: that war was all-consuming, that it forever altered the lives of those who fought in it, that it touched the ones left at home. That's the lesson of the row upon row of Legion markers in most large cemeteries. Read them and weep.

Another thing you can read in those rows is the pride that Canadians felt at being part of that war. Nowadays war is seen as something slightly tainted, a failure of diplomacy, but between 1939 and 1945, it was a patriotic duty, a task gladly accepted for home and country, a source of pride for families of the fighting men. They didn't have to apologize for their sons and daughters who went to war. They bragged about them and put their pictures front and centre on the piano in the front room. When those same sons and daughters, husbands and wives didn't come home, they mourned them deeply, but they had the comfort of knowing they had died for a cause, for something bigger than themselves.

"Proudly and lovingly remembered by his wife and children" is what it says on Sergeant John W. Fraser's marker in the Mount Pleasant Cemetery in Edmonton, along with the information that he died December 24, 1944, aged twenty-five years, eleven months, and that he is **"resting in Holland."** The Biblical verse about laying down one's life for one's friends appeared more than ever. Religion had taken something of a nose dive during the nasty thirties, but it came back with a vengeance during the war. Something had to make sense of the sacrifices. **"May his sacrifice bring peace on earth"** is the wish expressed on one marker in the Union Cemetery in Calgary. **"God took him home on his last flight,"** another explains. Other epitaphs call upon the Christian God to remember the promise of everlasting life. On Private Albert E. Sharpe's gravemarker are the words, **"Say Not Good Night But In Some Brighter Clime, Bid Me Good Morning."** Sharpe, a member of the 17th Battn. CEF., died November 11, 1945.

Trooper Joseph Adams died July 11, 1943, but his loved ones said on his gravemarker, **"They Are Not Dead, Our Loved Ones, They Are Waiting For us, On Beyond The Years."**

$\sim$

It took a few years after the war ended in 1945, but by the 1950s, western Canada was experiencing comparatively good times. Science and technology were the new gods, which may be why the old God was beginning to lose out in the graveyard. Fewer and fewer epitaphs referred to the Christian religion; they were replaced by neutral expressions such as **"The Reward of Toil is Rest," "Life's Work Well Done," "You Will Live Forever in Our Hearts,"** and **"Beyond the Sunset."**

This moving away from the sacred to the secular is epitomized in the symbol of hands. Hands on a gravemarker originally indicated a connection to the Christian God in one way or another: hands clasped horizontally meant a reunion of Heaven and earth; a single finger pointing upward indicated a trip heavenward; a single finger pointing down meant that God was giving special protection to the deceased. In the 1950s, the Praying Hands symbol began to appear, two hands holding a rosary or simply arranged in a praying mode. Although the image still had religious overtones, it revealed a subtle shift from God to people. God was still present but mostly as a court of appeal. Then came the image of two hands touching, the hands of a husband and wife, along with words like **"Together Forever"** or some such sentiment, and the shift was complete. The old religious connotation of hands was gone.

Sentiment was disappearing in the cemetery as well. It was in the 1950s that we got terribly businesslike in the graveyard and put the facts only on the markers — names and dates and not much else.

M.B. Byrnes, 1874-1959, is buried in the Grande Prairie graveyard. His marker says simply, **"Remembered as a Fine Gentleman."** And the MacLean grave in Three Hills tries to strike a happy medium, providing a little bit of information but nothing too mushy. Louise Margaret MacLean is remembered as a **"Pioneer R.N."** and Alexander Roderick MacLean is referred to as a **"Servant of All."** In many ways it is the quintessential 1950s gravemarker.

~

But the writing was on the wall. The next two decades, the 1960s and 1970s, became the most boring decades in Alberta's graveyard history. We didn't say much, and what's more, we had enough money to buy big black or grey granite markers to say nothing on. By this time, granite was the material of choice for gravestones. It was harder than either marble or the manmade materials and it took a design better, not that it mattered. We weren't into hearts and flowers — just facts.

Solon E. Low was a provincial politician for years, but he is buried at Cardston Cemetery without a word, just the dates 1900-62. In the Pine Lake Holy Trinity church graveyard is Arnold V. Hanson, 1911-78. His epitaph is a no-nonsense: **"Forever remembered by his friends and fellow curlers."**

Ernest Douglas Strand's tombstone in the Edson Cemetery is something of a mixed message. True to the times, the words are straightforward, not at all sentimental, but on the pedestal beside the white marble marker is a rather lovely white marble guardian angel, flowers in her hair, her hands raised in prayer. It's so unexpected that it makes you look twice.

In the 1960s and 1970s, we also got seriously into "memorial gardens." We would do anything, it seems, to avoid the idea of death, so we set up parks with names like Garden of Memories, and we buried one another in these places with only a flush bronze plaque to mark our place. That way, the cemetery didn't look like a cemetery; it just looked like a park with a suspicious lot of plastic flowers blowing in the wind. Then even the plastic flowers were outlawed, and the memorial gardens began to look like nothing. They were the ultimate denial of death. Interestingly, though, human nature began to reassert itself toward the end of the 1970s. Customers wanted upright markers, they wanted real flowers around the graves of their loved ones, they wanted the place to look like an honest-to-god cemetery because death was an honest-to-god event. Many of the memorial gardens, both private and municipal, eventually allowed some of the old-fashioned stuff back into their midst, not the least because weed whips came along. No longer did cemetery maintenance have to meet the needs of the mower before the needs of the mourner.

At the same time as we were hiding new deaths in memorial gardens, we began to take old deaths out of the closet and claim them for our own. Alberta communities were able to get government grants to clean up their old cemeteries, fence them, survey them, research names, put up cairns. Old cemeteries that had slumbered under weeds and neglect for years were rediscovered and put back on the map, cemeteries like the Prospy Cemetery in southern Alberta. It's a desolate piece of God's green earth, but it has a cairn on it now that lists the hardy folks who tried to make a go of it between 1914 and 1938. The final entries on the list are **"Baby Girl"** and **"The Unknown."**

An interest in genealogy enjoyed a revival in the 1970s as well. Families who hadn't given Uncle Harry a thought in years suddenly went in search of his grave and added him to their family tree files. Even if Uncle Harry had lived or died under unusual circumstances, families sought him out; there seemed to be a need for completion, continuity, belonging.

The grandson of a suicide victim came to the Willow Grove graveyard near St. Paul to try to find his grandfather's grave. He was from New York, had never been to Canada or known his grandfather, but he wanted to see and experience as much as he could. The small grey marker he came looking for was originally located outside the boundaries of the regular graveyard — as sometimes happened when suicide was considered a sin against God and the church — but by the time the young man came to the area, the graveyard had been cleaned up, and his grandfather was once again part of the community.

~

By the 1980s, we had come full circle, back to sentiment, to religion, to large markers, to unrestrained displays of emotion. Either that, or we went to the other extreme and didn't do any of the above, choosing instead to go the simplest route possible — cremation perhaps, or such a simple gravemarker as to be invisible. Society couldn't stand to be homogenous; neither, of course, could our graveyards.

The big monuments were a continuing sign of prosperity. People had more money and therefore could buy larger gravemarkers, if that happened to be their cultural and personal choice. What's more, we could put as many words and pictures on those big black markers as we could dream up because the technology came along to make it possible. No longer were the images applied by hand or by a fiddly sand blasting process. Computers had entered the picture, and processes such as photo etching or shadow toning could reproduce on granite actual scenes of the farm or a picture of a favourite horse or a mountain or a palm tree or just about anything you could imagine, within the limits of taste, and even those were stretched sometimes.

How far to go with modern expressions and understandings is

another development of the 1980s. The memorial makers tell me there is a gravemarker in Edmonton that says, **"She was a good lay."** I've kept an eye out for it, but I've not looked too hard. I'm a product of an earlier era when foolishness of that sort would not be countenanced in the graveyard. Yet, I guess, in this day and age of human rights, we have a right to say what we like in the graveyard. Who's to say nay? Calgary is supposed to have a gravemarker that says, **"That's the way the cookie crumbles."** I haven't found that one either.

Anyway, as a result of space age technology, a number of modern graves have fairly long poems or readings reproduced on them. **"Footprints"** is a favourite. Also the one that begins, **"Do not stand before me and weep..."** The Twenty-third Psalm is reproduced on several gravemarkers that I've seen, and Bible verses are again in vogue.

Some of the customized epitaphs I've found in graveyards lately include lines like: **"A Pioneer At Rest, His Last Furrow Plowed,"** **"A Tender Son and Faithful Friend — Gone Fishing,"** **"Brother, Golfer, Friend,"** **"Our Farmin' Truck Drivin' Daddy."**

But it's not the words, it's the pictures that have changed the graveyard more than anything in the last few years. For instance, the gravemarker of Cecil Turner, 1915-88, in Three Hills has a shadow tone picture of his actual truck on it with the words beneath it, **"Serving Highway 21 for Thirty Years."** It's a bit surprising at first, such a direct message, almost like an advertisement, and yet it tells the story. I can stand there in front of his tombstone and fill in the blanks — right or wrong — just as I used to do with the symbols and words on very early tombstones. They're just different symbols and words, that's all.

In Whitecourt, the gravemarker of Kenneth J. Robinson, 1943-80, has a picture of a hard hat and work boots etched into the black granite along with his name and dates. Tells something of his story, doesn't it?

John Armstrong's gravemarker in the Elnora Cemetery includes the picture of a team of horses pulling what looks to be a typically rickety farm wagon. On the seat of the wagon sits the ever-patient farmer, or at least that's what the picture tells me. The words tell me it's **"The End Of The Trail."** Taken together, the two create a sweet message, stronger than either one of them alone.

In the Hinton graveyard, Vans Havelock Hulbert, 1925-81, is pictured on his own marker. He is wearing a miner's lamp, a mountain scene

155

is depicted next to him, and the words say, **"He still leads the way."** Apparently Mr. Hulbert was a miner in his day, and since I was standing on a hilltop anyway, I looked across the valley to see if any of the mountains out there matched the one on the tombstone. Mountains don't make themselves easily recognizable, so it was hard to tell, but it occurred to me that, thanks to this brave new form of tombstone talk, I had looked up. I had tried to take the story one step further. Maybe there is no need to mourn the passing of words and stories on gravestones. We live in a world of images, after all. Those pictures in the graveyard may be the logical extension of a world where images are more important than words.

Thus, I warn you that coming soon to a graveyard near you, and coming more and more often, will be pictures of all sorts: photo etchings, shadow tone pictures, computer-aided drawings, and actual photographs preserved in various space age materials. Watch for them.

Cremation is another story of change that has begun to figure more prominently in our world over the last two decades, but even that change is undergoing changes. Cremation seemed so appropriate for a modern world. There is no arable land wasted for burial purposes, no going-in-debt to provide a tombstone, no religious fuss, no muss. But it didn't work as well as expected because people need some fuss, some sort of ceremony to mark a death, and after the death, they need a place to go. They need to be able to stand in front of something permanent and know that grandma is there. Funeral directors now recommend that cremains (the word for cremated remains) be scattered upon or buried within a family plot with at least a small footplate to identify the person. If remains are scattered, they recommend that a memorial plaque be mounted nearby.

Mind you, you can't do that if you decide to scatter ashes over a favourite lake or on a mountain top in a national park, the first choice of a lot of people. For one thing, the national parks aren't very keen on having people scatter human remains willy-nilly in the park. For another, the process often endangers the living. There are a number of stories about people who hire a plane so that they can scatter ashes over some perfect spot. Once they get there, they lean out of the plane to scatter the cremains to the four winds, only to have those same four winds return the ashes to the inside of the plane, where chaos reigns until the ashes settle. And finally, park people don't allow memorial plaques on the trees and mountains in their jurisdiction.

In other words, cremation requires a lot of thought and planning.

The Jasper Cemetery contains one solution to the problem. The Lewis family decided on cremation for their family members, but they also put a permanent marker in the cemetery with the words, "**Their ashes were spread over their favourite lake**."

In Edmonton's Mount Pleasant Cemetery, the Beach family went the same route — a gravemarker that remembers four members of one family, three of whom were cremated and scattered somewhere else, one who anchors the space. Future generations will thus have a place to go to when they want to remember.

Death, it seems, requires a place as much as life does.

The funeral industry is beginning to pick up on the problems associated with cremation, which is why they have begun to install columbaria in certain graveyards. A columbarium is a bank of granite and metal drawers with each drawer designed to hold the ashes of one or two individuals. They are generally placed among trees or clustered on the edge of the cemetery as if to de-emphasize the fact that they are essentially dresser drawers full of human ashes. The front of each drawer has just enough room for names and dates and not much more, the idea being that people who were previously willing to be scattered over a mountain top, lost to posterity forever, would not want a bunch of words or symbols or plastic flowers on their drawers. Wrong again. As long as there's somewhere to hang a flower or a wreath or a flag, they appear.

The Edmonton Evergreen Cemetery has several clusters of columbaria on its edges, all of them very tasteful arrangements of granite and bronze, but get closer and you will find plastic flowers, straw wreaths, a sheaf of wheat on individual drawers. We will not be denied our individuality.

There is one other method of "disposal." I don't like this rather clinical term, but my old friend who has selected this particular route tells me not to be silly. A body is just a body, he says, after life has departed. So why not donate it to a medical school where it will do some good? He has signed the papers with the University of Calgary allowing them the use of his body after death. They, in turn, have promised a proper burial and a standard flush marker bearing his name in Queen's Park Cemetery. Thus, my old friend is pleased to tell me, he'll do some good, and he won't cost anybody anything after death.

Still, I may go and put a flower on him now and then. He can't prevent that, and I may need it. We move along the spectrum of attitudes toward death at different speeds, and I admit I'm back there wanting a rock to talk to and a name to touch.

∼

I explored over 250 graveyards in the course of this research, and it didn't matter how big the graveyard or how beautiful or how ugly, for that matter, I was inevitably moved by the tombstones — the rocks — and what they stood for. It is hard to explain that reaction to people, and one day as I fretted about the words I needed to communicate my feelings, a line from a Robinson Jeffers poem jumped out at me: "History passes like falling rocks."

That seemed to me to be just about right. Agreed, I had rocks on the mind, both the tombstone kind and the ones that I saw along the mountain roads where I was continually warned of "Falling Rocks." But that line of poetry said what I was having trouble saying: history does pass like falling rocks. Something happens — a war, an accident, an illness, a death — and it falls to the road in front of us like a rock, stopping us in our tracks. Eventually we are able to get beyond it, to move the memory to the side of our lives and drive on. But the rock doesn't ever go away; the memory is still there.

And so it is with the "rocks" we leave behind in our cemeteries. The granite and marble, the flush bronze plaques and wooden crosses and, yes, even the blasted plastic flowers are reminders of journeys along the road. It is their job to hold still while everything else moves past and around them. To keep the faith and tell the story. To stand as a reminder of the life lived, the person loved.

∼

THE LAST WORD: From the Calgary gravemarker of George Park who "departed this transitory life in 1932."

Then think as slow and soft we tread
Among the solitary dead
Time was, like us, they life possessed
And time shall be when we shall rest.

∼

How to Explore a Graveyard

There are two main rules:

1 – Respect the graves and the people that they mark.

2 – Close the gates.

That's all you need to know if you're a casual visitor to graveyards. But if you want to do some research and get a bit more serious about graveyard exploring, you should also:

3 – Wear comfortable shoes, long pants and a hat.

4 – Take lunch.

5 – Take a camera and a notepad.

If you want to see a lot of graveyards and continue the research, you'd better:

6 – Choose a focus or a specialty; otherwise your family may begin to have conversations about you behind closed doors. However, if you establish a reason for your ramblings, you can say of a Sunday morning, "I'm off to do continuing research on sandstone markers of the late 19th century." See how sensible that sounds, how academic and almost necessary?

7 – If you're not sure what you want to research specifically in Alberta graveyards, start with your own family. Make charts. Find your own connections. Take pictures.

8 – Once you've got the hang of graveyard exploring, you'll likely find your own area of interest, but here are a few suggestions. Find everything you can that relates to the Northwest Rebellion of 1885, for instance. See how many different wars you can find reference to. Find unusual names. Do some arithmetic until you find the person who lived the longest. Study epitaphs. Study religious iconography. Find famous people.

9 – Enjoy the journey. Graveyards are often off the beaten path. You'll get to see parts of the province you never even knew existed.

10 – To fill in the blanks after you've done your exploring, get to know the people at local museums. They know all sorts of things. Read

local history books, haunt the local library, talk to oldtimers of the area. Also check in with the Alberta Genealogical Society, P.O. Box 12015, Edmonton, AB, T5J 3L2, or the Alberta Family Histories Society, P.O. Box 30270, Stn. B., Calgary, T2M 4P1. The Provincial Museum in Edmonton is also full of good material. Don't be afraid to ask.

Cemetery at St. Mary's Russian
Greek Orthodox Church near Nisku.

Index

Vulcan.....150

Wainwright.....126
Walsh, W.L.....62
Walton, Harold.....17
Wandering Spirit.....113
Whitecourt.....108, 155
Wildwood.....86
Willingdon.....80

Williscroft, John.....113
Willow Grove....154

Yeoman, Emily.....22
Yet, Wong.....86

Zengel, Raphael.....124